Arthur Koestler

Titles in the series Critical Lives present the work of leading cultural figures of the modern period. Each book explores the life of the artist, writer, philosopher or architect in question and relates it to their major works.

In the same series

Arthur Koestler

Edward Saunders

REAKTION BOOKS

For my parents

Published by Reaktion Books Ltd
Unit 32, Waterside
44–48 Wharf Road
London N1 7UX, UK
www.reaktionbooks.co.uk

First published 2017

This book was written on behalf of the Ludwig Boltzmann Gesellschaft as part of the research programme of the Ludwig Boltzmann Institute for the History and Theory of Biography.

Ludwig Boltzmann Institut
Geschichte und Theorie der Biographie

Printed and bound in Great Britain by Bell & Bain, Glasgow

A catalogue record for this book is available from the British Library

ISBN 978 1 78023 716 9

Contents

Abbreviations

Arthur Koestler, 1940. Portrait by Gisèle Freund.

Introduction: Why Koestler?

All the mystery in life turns out to be this same mystery, the join
between things which are distinct and yet continuous, body and
mind, free will and causality, living cells and life itself.
From *Hapgood* (1988) by Tom Stoppard

'If any living writer is still being read in a hundred years' time,
that writer will surely be Arthur Koestler. For no one has lived so
fully and intensely a uniquely twentieth-century experience, and
produced books which give the feel of what it has all been like.'
These are the words of the British intellectual historian Maurice
Cranston, reviewing the first biography of Arthur Koestler for
the *American Spectator* in 1983, shortly after Koestler's death.[1]
As his words show, Arthur Koestler was more than just a famous
journalist: he was a witness to several of the most important
episodes in twentieth-century European history and was acquainted
with the leading intellectual, literary and political figures of his age.
Yet he was always an outsider. Born into the Austro-Hungarian
secular Jewish middle classes, he belonged everywhere and nowhere
in the post-1918 world. He never found a single, defining thread that
would provide orientation. Koestler became famous through his
commitment to progressive causes but later changed direction
and developed decidedly esoteric interests.

Although he was well read in literature and wrote a series
of novels, his main interests were contemporary politics, science

and psychology. His greatest achievement is commonly believed to be the anti-totalitarian novel *Darkness at Noon* (1940), yet Koestler wrote in a broad range of genres, from autobiography to political essays and popular science works. In the same review, Cranston, who was clearly a fan, called Koestler's *The Sleepwalkers* (1959) 'a masterpiece', and compared his scientific criticism favourably to the work of Karl Popper.[2] However, Koestler's productivity did not always lead to acclaim and many of his books, particularly the later ones, were critical failures. In particular, Koestler's later interests in eccentric subjects such as the paranormal were laughed at by some. His suicide pact with his much younger wife Cynthia in 1983 was widely criticized and the posthumous rape claim that followed caused further reputational damage.

Koestler was a one-time cause célèbre who became a pariah. The rape claim has proven especially divisive. There are many other reasons to criticize Koestler and even to dislike him. His life story is not always edifying, but this does not mean his life or work should be ignored or forgotten. He was a fearless and forthright voice on many issues that remain of relevance today. He had a passion for communicating ideas that is visible throughout his work and led a life that was often controversial and rarely boring. Even if it is impossible to wholeheartedly endorse his example (which was, in former times, the biographer's task), Koestler was nevertheless an impulsive, engaging and highly original figure in whose life and work there is much to admire. Koestler was far more than a 'self-promoting smart-arse', as the author Tibor Fischer has described him.[3] He was an often pitch-perfect and incisive commentator on twentieth-century life, with a remarkable talent for literary autobiography.

Autobiography is at the heart of Koestler's work. As every writer on Koestler notes, he saw the value in his life story as that of 'the typical case-history of a Central European member of the intelligentsia in the totalitarian age' (*IW*, p. 428). It was a bold claim, but one which betrayed more about his political purposes than his egotism. His point was that for an entire generation of Europeans in the mid-twentieth century, geographical displacement, radical political affiliations, political discrimination and even imprisonment and exile were 'normal' experiences. Koestler wrote both volumes of his autobiography *Arrow in the Blue* (1952) and *The Invisible Writing* (1954) for English-speaking audiences familiar with the economic and human costs of war, but largely untouched by the broader social and cultural consequences of totalitarianism and the fight against it. As he emphasized, he was more interested in being a chronicler of his times than being a self-portraitist.

Rather than calling him a 'life-writer', though, I prefer to call him a 'documentarist', for his fictional works also contain valuable insights into the impact of global politics on individual lives. In his fiction, Koestler transformed and elaborated his life experiences, as well as those of others, into political allegories. *Darkness at Noon*, his best-known work, describes the interrogation of a political prisoner in the Soviet Union. Koestler had visited the Soviet Union and had been on death row in Spain; close friends of his were imprisoned by Stalin, while the main character, Rubashov, was named after a man Koestler had met in Palestine. The novel *Arrival and Departure* (1943) depicts the experience of travelling into political exile via Lisbon, while *Thieves in the Night* (1946) is set in a Zionist kibbutz, the kind that Koestler had attempted to join in the 1920s. In his fiction, as in his autobiographies, Koestler was eager to document not only historical contexts and events, but questions and political debates. To some extent his fiction also describes the experiences he did not have, representative moments of twentieth-century history where he could use personal insight as ersatz first-hand experience.

Experience was, however, not something he lacked. While still a boy he experienced the short-lived Hungarian Commune of 1919; lived in Austria during its fledgling years as a democracy; witnessed the attempts to establish a Jewish state in British Mandate Palestine;

worked as a correspondent in Paris; and experienced the high life in Weimar-era Berlin. As if living out a series of historical tableaux, he experienced the rise of Nazism; saw (or pretended not to see) the terrible consequences of the Ukrainian famine, or Holodomor; infiltrated the Nationalist camp during the Spanish Civil War; and was imprisoned both in Franco's Spain and in wartime France, before escaping into exile in the United Kingdom. There he would later discover that many of his relatives had died in the Holocaust. He spent periods living in Wales, France and the United States, before settling in London, with a second home in Austria and later in East Anglia. Throughout much of this time he had an incredibly complicated love life, often carried on outside his serious relationships (of which there were between four and six, depending on how they are defined, but including three marriages). In later years, he involved himself in humanitarian causes such as the abolition of capital punishment, turned to science writing, and explored interests in psychology and the paranormal. In the decade leading up to his suicide he became an advocate of euthanasia, and, by committing suicide, ended his life in a characteristically statemental way.

Koestler's life and work is a journey from *fin-de-siècle* Budapest, via Vienna in the 1920s, to the roots of the Israel–Palestine conflict. He involved himself on both sides of the story of Communism and anti-Communism in Europe and became an important cultural commentator during the Cold War. Unlike many other exiles, Koestler had little difficulty establishing himself in the intellectual elites of Britain and France. His vocational interest in popular science took him in new directions at a time when the 'Two Cultures' debate had begun in earnest. Aside from his dabbling in more wacky topics such as ufology and magic mushrooms, Koestler was also far-sighted in his commitment to prison arts, and was the first sponsor of a competition that still bears his name: the Koestler Awards.

Koestler's life-writing and his literary reputation are interdependent and in the development of the latter the influence and absence of his autobiographical gifts are clear. While Koestler's story of his youth and early career makes compelling reading, it is regrettable that he did not tell the story of the second half of his life. If he had, his conceptual work might have found a more receptive audience, or at least one which was able to make sense of where his ideas came from. No doubt to his chagrin, his reputation was never based on any personal philosophical system, which is why he has often been described as a journalist. He was a popularizer of ideas who succeeded repeatedly in structuring debates, or, in modern media parlance, of framing the public conversation. He achieved this through a talent for vivid description and an understanding of metaphor. While Koestler is primarily associated with other famous left-wing writers, such as his friend George Orwell, in some ways he was closer in spirit to the celebrity radio or television presenter of today, an idiosyncratic Cold War talking head. The big cultural debates in which he took part were rarely frivolous and many are still relevant today. To his contemporaries Arthur Koestler was significant because in an age of ideology and radical nationalism, he symbolized Europeanism and humanism.

When I began working on Koestler, I found it difficult to get an easy grasp of his life and work, despite of (or, just possibly, because of) the lengthy and detailed biographies that already exist. Opinion on Koestler is also split, as an unpleasant dispute followed the publication of David Cesarani's 'unauthorized' biography in 1998, which was widely perceived as a debunking.[4] This Critical Life is intended to present Koestler to new audiences and to provide a concise introduction into the impressive range of his work. It is based on existing biographical information and is indebted to the studies by Michael Scammell and others. The intention here is not to revolutionize understanding of Koestler, although I hope to provide a fresh take, but rather to give a balanced and concise account, in particular one which pays attention to Koestler's own crafting of his public persona, whether as a science writer, a novelist or an autobiographer, without whitewashing the more troubling aspects of his private life.

1

From Budapest to Palestine

The first part of Koestler's life is an extraordinary tale, partly because he told it so well. Koestler was born on the afternoon of 5 September 1905 in Budapest, in the Austro-Hungarian Empire, as the only child of Austrian and Hungarian Jewish parents. His was an upper-middle-class, bilingual childhood in the heart of a multi-ethnic conservative nation that was shot through with a commitment to radicalism and progress.[1] At least outwardly liberal, Budapest was a self-consciously modernizing city and the family's apartment was located only metres from the route of the city's 1896 underground line, now Metro 1, which runs beneath Andrássy Avenue, Budapest's answer to the Champs-Elysées. What it was not, however, was Vienna – a fact much lamented by Koestler's Austrian-Jewish mother, Adele, who felt she had been born to better things.

Very short, with brown hair and blue eyes, Koestler was a lonely child and craved the company of his peers. He disliked his mother, who coped badly with him, and was distant from his father, Henrik, although he later remembered him kindly. Henrik was a businessman, prone to mad entrepreneurial ventures promising a quick fortune, such as the giant letter-opening device he proudly exhibited to his family one day in 1910 or 1911 (*AB*, p. 23). Koestler's mother was a temperamental, controlling figure who believed children needed discipline and enforced a Victorian programme of rules and penalties, implemented in practice by Bertha, the tyrannical maid (*AB*, pp. 33–4).

A progressive childhood: Laura Polanyi-Striker's kindergarten in Budapest, *c.* 1911.

This, at least, was Koestler's view, presented in his autobiography, *Arrow in the Blue*. Evidence to the contrary is suggested by the fact that Adele, the descendant of one of Vienna's leading Jewish families, sent her son to a progressive kindergarten on Andrássy Avenue run by Laura Striker (also known as 'Mausi'), of the Polanyi or Pollacsek family, who was firmly part of the Hungarian cultural and political establishment and closely connected to some of the leading thinkers, composers and artists of the day. In 1904, Striker had been the first woman to complete a doctorate in history at Budapest University and, had circumstances not prevented her, might have become an academic herself, like her more famous brothers Karl and Michael Polanyi. Her kindergarten focused on the arts and on play and, incorporating Freudian ideas, for the children clothing was optional.[2] It was here that Koestler met Eva, Laura Striker's daughter, with whom, years later, he would have one of his most decisive friendships.

After kindergarten Arthur was sent to a Hungarian-language school (not a German one). While his father was a native speaker of Hungarian, Koestler grew up speaking several languages because

Koestler's mother spoke German to him at home, and his parents employed French and English governesses. He claimed reading was discouraged by his parents, but in truth a huge range of books was available to him and he read them voraciously. With servants and a good address, he had a highly privileged early childhood, even if he did not enjoy it.

The surname Koestler was, in a way, Arthur's own invention. In Hungarian it could be spelled Kőstler, although his Hungarian passport in the 1940s gave the name 'Arthur Kestler', and his registration documents in Vienna in the 1920s 'Arthur Köstler'. 'Koestler' was an alternate spelling of 'Köstler', the German version of the name without an umlaut, which Arthur made his signature as an aspiring journalist in 1926.[3] Arthur claimed that the surname had been assumed by his grandfather, who kept his true identity concealed from his family (AB, p. 19). However, flexibility with names was not unusual. In Habsburg Hungary many people were bilingual in Hungarian and German and it was common to spell one's name differently according to which language was being spoken. There was also political pressure in the late nineteenth century to 'Magyarize' non-Hungarian family names.

Koestler's mysterious grandfather Leopold/Lipot was alleged to have fled from the Crimean War or political persecution to settle in Hungary. This story has since been dismissed as legend, though it is tempting to believe that this mysterious grandfather really did come from the Russian Empire. Michael Scammell has shown that Lipot served in the Hungarian Army, but where he came from before that is open to speculation. Much more is known about Adele's family, though, whom Koestler disguised as the 'Hitzigs' in his autobiography. They were in fact called Jeiteles, a famous Jewish family with many worthy if hardly world-famous forebears.[4] His maternal grandfather, Jacob Jeiteles, had left Austria for New York in the 1890s, having been ruined in a financial scandal: another curious figure in the family album.

Koestler had an ambiguous view on his Jewish heritage. Although he would join a Zionist fraternity while studying in Vienna, and attempt to join a kibbutz in 1920s Palestine, Koestler also went out of his way to distance himself from Judaism. In midlife he played down its role in his childhood. For example, in the first volume of his autobiography, *Arrow in the Blue*, Koestler relates a story in which his grandfather Leopold/Lipot, who could not bring himself to break the kosher diet of his childhood, on a regular basis buys Arthur a ham sandwich to eat. The ham sandwich is a symbol of 'enlightened' secularism and a clear statement of distance from the Jewish religion. In the same book, Koestler alludes to a lack of awareness about Jewish life in his youth, but does not give many specifics. Instead, he compares the Jewish experience to that of all other minorities, suggesting that perceived shared Jewish characteristics stem from a history of oppression (*AB*, pp. 102–3).

If Koestler later seemed to play down his Jewish origins, it may be because Jewishness was not the exception in his childhood world; it was still a kind of norm. But in later life, he compared the account in George Clare's *Last Waltz in Vienna: The Destruction of a Family, 1842–1942* (1982) to his own family's experience.[5] Clare describes how all Central European Jews suffered from a deep sense of inequality: 'We wore fine clothes, had access even to titles and dignities, possessed influence and wealth. But full equality, inner equality, still eluded us.'[6]

In 1900, shortly before Koestler's birth, one-fifth of Budapest's population was Jewish. Most had German family names, due to earlier policies of Germanization, and few were Orthodox or Yiddish-speaking (indeed, assimilated German-speaking Jews often looked down on those who did speak Yiddish).[7] There were parts of the city, such as the central Leopold District of Pest, close to where Koestler grew up, where this population was highly concentrated. Although trouble was brewing, anti-Semitism was not yet a major phenomenon.[8] Moreover, the Moorish-style Dohány Street

Synagogue, the largest in Europe, was less than a thirty-minute walk from the Koestler apartment.

To some commentators (notably David Cesarani) the Jewishness of his childhood world seems oddly absent from Koestler's autobiographies. Steven Beller has suggested that members of the Jewish bourgeoisie were discriminated against in late Habsburg Austria, 'whether its members were willing to admit as much or not'.[9] But as Christian Buckard has put it, for Koestler Jewishness was not a political identity or lifestyle, but a religion (and one which his family did not practise).[10] Similarly, Koestler's first biographer, Iain Hamilton, has written that it was 'a matter of no great consequence'.[11] But perhaps the most helpful way of considering the question of Judaism in Koestler's life is to follow Lisa Silverman's comparison of Jewish identities to gender identities. Instead of looking for essential Jewishness in Koestler's life and work, we should pay attention to his engagement with the topic of being Jewish.[12] On an abstract or political level, Judaism did play an important part in Koestler's life, not least because of his Zionist involvement from his student days onwards, and it was the topic of several of his books. It would also be the source of numerous controversies. Later in life, Koestler would assert that Jews should either move to Israel or assimilate, and in his study of the Khazars he claimed that many European Jews had no Semitic heritage at all.

Koestler was often only a temporary resident of Budapest while he was growing up. The outbreak of the First World War had a negative impact on Henrik's business; Arthur's parents gave up their Budapest apartment and moved to Vienna. They would never have a fixed family home again. In Vienna the family lived in a succession of guesthouses. This got off to a bad start when the young Koestler managed to burn out several rooms in a hotel on Vienna's central square, Stephansplatz, having been left unattended with candles and matches. When an exploding tin of beans knocked him unconscious in the same hotel shortly afterwards, Koestler developed a reputation for extraordinary gifts (or so he claimed), and was under demand to assist in the then-popular table-lifting illusion – a premonition of esoteric interests later in life.

Around the same time, Koestler also had the first of a series of semi-spiritual experiences. He was overcome by an 'oceanic' feeling of the beauty of the world while being driven through the Hofburg Palace in an ambulance. Snow was falling, the sun was still shining, and he was overwhelmed by the beauty of the moment. He remembered 'the feeling of one's self peacefully dissolving in nature as a grain of salt dissolves in the ocean' (*AB*, pp. 39–40).

Arthur returned alone to Budapest in the autumn of 1915 to resume his schooling. Aged eleven, he lived most of the time with his Aunt Rosa (his mother's older sister) and Uncle Siegfried and their three children.[13] Koestler was an able pupil who did well at school. He attended the Hungarian equivalent of the Austrian *Realschule*, which had an emphasis on the sciences and languages that matched his interests. His favourite hobby was chess. For the rest of the war, his parents did a lot of travelling: his father on business in Hungary, his mother to and fro from Vienna. They continued to live in guesthouses.

As a schoolboy in Budapest, Arthur experienced both the Aster Revolution of November 1918, which saw the end of Habsburg rule in Hungary, and the March Revolution of 1919 that established the short-lived Hungarian Republic of Councils. He had vivid memories of both events. The attempt to transform Hungary into a socialist state meant that new teachers were brought into Koestler's school, who talked of economics, constitutional government and the hardships of rural life (*AB*, p. 62). Arthur's cousin Margit took the thirteen-year-old Arthur with her to a metal works, where she was teaching a course on political economy. Koestler later said that the experience of seeing grown men desperate for knowledge left him

A view of Stephansplatz, Vienna, 1914. The Koestler family stayed
at Stock-im-Eisen-Platz 3 (centre).

with a profound belief in free universal education, irrespective
of parental income (*AB*, p. 66).

That summer Arthur had a second semi-spiritual experience
which later inspired the title of the first volume of his autobiography,
Arrow in the Blue. The incident occurred while he was staring into
a clear blue sky, lying on a hill in Budapest. He imagined shooting
a 'super-arrow' into space, which would travel for infinity without
stopping. Elated by the beauty of the sky, he found this idea almost
incomprehensible, and was struck by a sense of injustice at not
being able to understand the nature of eternity, 'one's most sacred
right – the right to know'. Eternal motion seemed to imply the
impossibility of knowledge and to prevent understanding of why
humans were there to witness it in the first place (*AB*, pp. 51–2).
From the question of the nature of existence, he had begun to ask
why there is life in the first place. In Koestler's autobiography, it
is the first hint towards what Richard Freadman calls Koestler's
'scientistic mysticism'.[14]

However, Koestler's contemplation of blue, Communist skies in search of the infinite did not continue undisturbed. The Republic of Councils was brought down by August and, like many others, the Koestler family fled the approaching Romanian Army. Travelling through a country in turmoil, they resorted to bribes to get themselves out of trouble and made it across the border into Austria. From there they proceeded once again to Vienna.[15]

While the political situation in Hungary remained unstable, Arthur was sent to an exclusive and expensive secondary school in Baden, a spa town sixteen miles south of Vienna, having passed a competitive entrance exam. At first, the Koestler family were not financially affected by exile; on the contrary, Henrik's business boomed and for a time the family lived in a suite at the Grand Hotel, one of the luxurious Ringstraße hotels near the Vienna State Opera. After a year, however, the fifteen-year-old Arthur was sent to live at a boarding house for boys in Baden whose members were predominantly Jewish. Short and slight, although elegantly dressed, Koestler was an insecure and unhappy teenager and did not enjoy his time at school. Apart from living out his insecurities, Arthur began to be more aware of his Jewish and Hungarian heritage and, despite rising anti-Semitism in Hungary, visited Lake Balaton with his father more than once.[16] It was at the boarding house that he probably had his first sexual experiences, with the maid, Mathilda (*AB*, p. 77).

His parents continued to travel. Koestler would later hint that he knew more about his parents' personal life than he should have and it is clear that the marriage had broken down to a degree. Both Adele and Henrik may have had affairs and Adele left a curious note about Arthur in her diary: 'I taught you to speak, you teach me to be silent.'[17] The frequent absence of his parents was probably hard for Arthur as well, not to mention their ever-changing fortunes. By 1922 the Koestler family was living more modestly in Pension Luisenheim, at Eisengasse 2 (now

Wilhelm-Exner-Gasse), very close to the 'Gürtel' ('the belt'), the ring-road and elevated railway that separates the bourgeois 'inner districts' of Vienna from the neighbourhoods beyond. Excluding the summer holidays, Koestler lived here from September 1922 until March 1926. By coincidence, it was the same guesthouse that Theodor Adorno would choose when he moved to Vienna in 1925, aged 21, having completed his doctorate. Koestler met him briefly once at breakfast.

In the summer of 1922, aged sixteen, Arthur finished school. He proceeded to apply for a place to study engineering at the prestigious Higher School of Technology on Vienna's Karlsplatz, today the Vienna University of Technology. After his seventeenth birthday in September, Koestler joined a Zionist fraternity called Unitas, on the recommendation of his mother. Such fraternities were chiefly devoted to drinking and duelling, but a canny and well-connected friend of the family told Adele at a tea party that Unitas would help keep Arthur out of trouble. Adele thought it involved improving cultural activities and Koestler claimed that neither he nor his parents knew anything of Zionism (*AB*, p. 85).

Whether aware of Zionist politics or not (complete ignorance seems unlikely), Koestler's initially naive involvement in Unitas would change his life, as it was this involvement that would take him to Palestine and launch his career as a journalist. The Unitas fraternity was elitist and its members were largely privileged Jewish students from the University of Vienna. It was by no means less rowdy than its rivals. Koestler described how Jewish fraternities overcompensated for any perceived weakness in relation to the Pan-German and Liberal fraternities. By the 1920s anti-Semitism among the Nationalist Pan-German organizations meant that traditional Saturday parades at the university descended regularly into fistfights (*AB*, p. 83). The fighting, of course, was followed by drinking, and fraternity life also involved the frequent seduction of working-class girls.

For the lonely and unhappy teenager it was the camaraderie of a fraternity that was the most welcome change. He gradually became drawn into political Zionism which for him, as for Theodor Herzl, was a matter of national identity, not a religious question.[18] In his second year at university Koestler became the president of the Unitas fraternity and chair of all the Zionist fraternities in Vienna, and in the spring of 1924 he presided over a ball for them at the Hofburg Palace. Surrounded by friends and able to enjoy all the city had to offer, Koestler later described these years as the happiest of his life (*AB*, p. 95). He spent the rest of his time reading about psychology and neglected his engineering studies. It was also at this time that Koestler fell under the influence of Wolfgang von Weisl, a Zionist campaigner and an advocate of Revisionist Zionism, which was the campaign to create a Zionist state, not just a 'national home', in Palestine. Von Weisl became one of Koestler's closest friends.

It was during these busy, happy months that the nineteen-year-old Koestler had a third semi-mystical experience, only a stone's throw away from the location of the first. He was in Vienna's Volksgarten park reading gruesome accounts of anti-Semitic violence by Arabs in British Mandate Palestine – the kind of thing, as he would write much later, euphemistically termed 'disturbances' (*PF*, p. 18). It may have been an account of the 1921 Arab riots which originated in Jaffa, where Jews were brutally killed and raped in an immigrant hostel, leading to the death of 47 Jews and 48 Arabs.[19] Filled with outrage, he opened a book on the theory of relativity instead. Reading it, he was overcome by an opposing feeling of wonder and calm. Describing these conflicting emotions later, he compared them to his earlier image of the super-arrow fired into infinity. Now the arrow was split in two, travelling in opposite directions. His feeling of moral indignation about the Jewish situation was counteracted by an 'oceanic' feeling of mystical wonder at 'rocks decaying into swamps, and primeval forests being transformed into coal' (*AB*, pp. 97–8).

Even if Koestler still retained his scientific and aesthetic interests, his political involvement increased. In May 1924, as president of Unitas, Koestler was sent to greet Ze'ev Jabotinsky in Břeclav, on the Austrian-Czech border. A Russian Jewish novelist, journalist and the political leader of Revisionist Zionism, Jabotinsky was the one who would convert Koestler fully to the cause. Even before Jabotinsky's arrival, Koestler had been able to convince all the Jewish fraternities in Vienna to endorse a Zionist state.[20] Jabotinsky gave two speeches at Vienna's Konzerthaus (not at the 'Kursaal', as Koestler confusingly wrote in *Arrow in the Blue*) on 24 May and 28 May 1924 on the topics 'Islam, Europe and the Jews' and 'The Crisis in Zionism'.[21] To give some impression of the venue, this famous Viennese concert hall was then only a decade old and had a capacity of well over a thousand. Karl Kraus was a regular and read from his own works there only two days later.[22] Jabotinsky made a deep impression on Koestler, who accompanied him to Czechoslovakia on the next leg of his lecture tour as an assistant.

Back in Vienna, with his engineering studies all but forgotten, Koestler became involved with HeChaver ('Comrade' in Hebrew), an association for Jews from the former Russian Empire, and became something of a Russophile.[23] He wrote a first article for a Zionist newspaper, *Wiener Morgenzeitung*, and attended major Zionist meetings in Paris and Vienna. At this time Koestler was still living at the Pension Luisenheim, but not all was well with the Koestler family. Sometime in 1924 or 1925, Henrik was bankrupted by his business partner, who had been committing financial fraud for two years. This resulted in a long and unsuccessful legal battle that spelled the end of the Koestler family's prosperity and his father's health. In the summer of 1924, however, they holidayed in the Alpine resort of Pertisau am Achensee, staying at the fifteenth-century Fürstenhaus hotel.[24]

The failure of the business put additional pressure on Koestler to complete his engineering studies and secure himself a livelihood.

However, while his parents were away in England in late 1925 attempting to rescue what was left of the business, Koestler made a radical decision. One of his friends from HeChaver, a Russian man called Orokhov, argued with him about free will. In an impetuous attempt to prove that he could indeed determine his future, Koestler decided to burn his matriculation book, which was the definitive record of his studies. It was a rainy October night and, having walked home to the Pension Luisenheim, he proceeded to do so. He had almost finished university, but could no longer take his degree. Faced with the first major impasse in his life, against the advice of his friends, and having lied in letters to his parents about his intentions, Koestler decided to go to Palestine as a pioneer. Opinion is split as to whether Koestler's account is reliable. Was he really just trying to escape or was this, as Cesarani has suggested, the kind of political stunt his mentor Jabotinsky was trying to encourage?[25]

There were certainly numerous factors in Koestler's decision. The evidence suggests that late in 1925 Jabotinsky had a different future

A Koestler holiday destination in 1924. Hotel Fürstenhaus, Pertisau am Achensee, Austria.

in mind for Koestler, whom he described in a letter as 'handsome, *charming manners*, clever, etc.', considering him as a possible future secretary. Jabotinsky was undecided whether to persuade Koestler to move – presumably to Paris, where Jabotinsky had founded the Union of Zionist Revisionists in April that year – despite Koestler's obvious enthusiasm.[26] Combined with Koestler's irresistible attraction to a cause, the new financial pressure on the family and, no doubt, some degree of late adolescent pique, it may have felt easy to him to justify the decision to go to Palestine. Either way, Cesarani is right that the way Koestler tells the story plays down other contextual factors, such as the growing anti-Semitism of 1920s Vienna and his own Jewish background.[27] Koestler learned enough Modern Hebrew to pass an exam and was able to use Zionist connections to obtain an immigration certificate. He left Vienna by train on 1 April 1926, and was waved off by the members of Unitas singing 'Hatikvah', the melancholic Zionist song that would become the Israeli national anthem. He was twenty years old.

2

Zionist and Communist

Having escaped the prospect of becoming a Viennese engineer, Koestler felt liberated. However, on arrival at a small kibbutz (or *kvutsa*) in the Jezreel Valley, in the north of modern Israel, he discovered that he was not cut out for agricultural work. Kibbutz life in the mid-1920s was idealistic, socialist and required hard labour. Despite his practical mindset and certain nascent socialist sympathies, Koestler did not fit in and, after a month, the kibbutz informed him he would not be accepted. Koestler walked back to Haifa by foot. There Koestler found shelter in the home of Abram Weinshall, a Revisionist Party activist from Baku, and his Russian wife Zina. He helped Weinshall to set up a newspaper, a press agency and a legal aid resource. After a few weeks, an article by Koestler was picked up by the *Jüdische Rundschau*, a Zionist newspaper with a circulation of 10,000 in 1926.[1] Leaving the Weinshalls' home, Koestler lived in a state of poverty and could barely feed himself. He shared a room with a brother and sister from Russia and subsisted on coffee, bread and olives (*AB*, p. 137). After a stint as an architect lasting only a few weeks and having failed to make it as a lemonade seller, Koestler found himself slumming it in Haifa. A series of floors and sofas followed before Koestler's money finally ran out.

After four days without food, Koestler was saved by the unexpected arrival of Wolfgang von Weisl, the Zionist campaigner who had so inspired him in Vienna. Von Weisl was now a journalist for the Ullstein group, then a major independent publisher of books and newspapers based in Berlin. The following day he ran into an acquaintance from his school days on the beach and discovered that an article he had written had been printed, with some string-pulling by Adele, on the front page of the *Neue Freie Presse*, then one of Austria's leading newspapers. With this astonishing break, his career as a journalist began. Soon afterwards, Koestler left Haifa for Tel Aviv to make a fresh start and to develop the press agency. He did not make a triumphant arrival. To save money, he decided to walk.

Koestler lived in shared rooms in Tel Aviv and after a few false starts found a job selling advertising space for a magazine. Before he turned 21 in September, Koestler took in the atmosphere of the young city, but his press agency idea failed to take off. For a while it seemed as though he was making no progress, but Wolfgang von Weisl came to the rescue again. He asked Koestler to help him edit a trade publication in German and Arabic, to be published in Cairo. It lasted for a few months, but soon the prospect of a better job in the Revisionist Zionist movement came up in Berlin. He travelled there via Budapest, where he was able to see his parents and place some of his unpublished articles with the German-language paper *Pester Lloyd*. Adele and Henrik were newly returned to Budapest and living in a furnished room in order to save money. It must have been a disappointment for the once fashionable couple.

Koestler's lot was not much better. Given how exciting Berlin is fabled to have been in the 1920s, Koestler's first experience of it in 1927 was decidedly negative. His job in Zionist politics paid terribly and left him with no disposable income. He took a room near Alexanderplatz and knew only two people in the city: his boss and his mother's brother, Uncle Otto. It turned out to be a prelude to greater things, for within months Koestler had been nominated by von Weisl as his replacement as the Middle East correspondent for the Ullstein newspapers, home to some of Weimar Germany's most influential and widely read titles. This was a spectacular opportunity and a huge favour by von Weisl to Koestler. Koestler took a train to Vienna and secured a supplementary contract to write articles for the *Neue Freie Presse*. Being too self-effacing to ask his employers for a cash advance, Koestler sold his old books to raise money for his journey to Jerusalem and Adele even pawned her last remaining diamond ring.

The Jerusalem post led Koestler to meet, from the age of just 22, many of the most important figures in Middle East politics of the time, including the brothers King Faisal I of Iraq and Emir Abdullah I of Transjordan (later king of Jordan). After Ze'ev Jabotinsky came to Jerusalem in 1928, Koestler became a member of the editorial board of the Hebrew paper *Doar Hayom* (Daily Mail), a sensationalist right-wing daily.[2] Koestler had a weekend page in the paper and claimed to have introduced the first crossword puzzle in Hebrew, dubbed 'Brain Acrobatics' (*AB*, p. 183). With his salary from Ullstein and his income from his other work, Koestler was now able to support his parents financially and still live comfortably himself. Disaster was averted and his journalism career in the Middle East seemed likely to thrive. He even acquired a Palestinian passport (issued by the British government). Soon, though, his enthusiasm began to wane.

Koestler stayed in the Jerusalem post from the autumn of 1927 until the summer of 1929, when he requested a new position with the Ullstein company. He was tired of the atmosphere of Mandate Palestine and the pressure to speak Hebrew in the Zionist community. As someone who wrote for a living, this was more than a superficial consideration.[3] He was in luck: Ullstein sent him to Paris. It was another significant posting, as his predecessors had been none other than Kurt Tucholsky and Alfred Kantorowicz. He had chosen a good time to leave Jerusalem. In August 1929, 133 Jews and 116 Arabs were killed, and hundreds more on both sides were injured, in riots over access to the Western Wall, triggered by a squabble over the right to pray.[4]

In Paris, the job was more menial than that in Jerusalem. Arriving in July, the 24-year-old Koestler spent most of his time writing press summaries for Ullstein in regimented shifts and wrote feature articles on culture and science for the *Vossische Zeitung* in his spare time. He maintained a loose association with the Zionists, but did not continue working for the Revisionist movement, even though their headquarters were there. Shift work meant that Koestler's Paris was never a city of glamourous leisure; instead it was defined by the metro at rush hour, hard work in crowded basement offices and breakfasts at 3 am. Though he was socially isolated for much of his first stay there, Koestler learned to love the city and, when working early shifts, got to know its seedy underworld by frequenting all-night cafés and, often enough, the brothels. No stay in Paris would be complete without a passionate affair or two, and Koestler's lovers at this time included the Ullstein office secretary, a Viennese woman called Ingeborg Seidler, as well as a long-lost childhood friend from Budapest days, the potter Eva Striker (later famous as Eva Zeisel), who spent three months in the city. Mamaine Koestler would later refer to Eva as his first 'wife'.[5] An artist by disposition with an interest in Surrealism and Dada, Eva was on vacation from a majolica factory in Schramberg in Germany's Black Forest, where she was working as an industrial designer.[6]

A year on, Koestler was back in Berlin, where he continued to lead a bohemian personal life. This time he was able to enjoy the city properly. Eva was there too, living with her brother in an apartment rented from the Expressionist painter Emil Nolde in the city's then fashionable 'New West', and through them Koestler was well-connected with the left-wing Hungarian community in Berlin. Eva described the city as 'buzzing with contradictions, obsessed with modernity and urgency'.[7]

At Ullstein, Koestler was thought to have a gift for popular science writing, having interviewed the 1929 winner of the Nobel

A rare drawing of Koestler by Eva Striker (Eva Zeisel), *c.* 1930.

Prize in Physics, Louis de Broglie, while in Paris, and been appointed science editor for the Ullstein papers. This was a prestigious job which also meant more pay, although by his own account he was an insecure and aggressive personality at this age and rarely relaxed in professional contexts. He maintained that no one took him seriously, despite his obvious competence. He was a dreamer who did not quite fit in (*AB*, pp. 212–13). However, Koestler found that he had a greater passion for science writing than he did for international politics, and his new job came as a welcome change after his postings in Jerusalem and Paris. He interviewed Einstein by phone and wrote on the most exciting developments in atomic physics, some of which were happening in Berlin (*AB*, pp. 255–6). Koestler saw science and technology as an essential part of any education and lamented the disregard of it by most supposedly 'cultured' people. One of his most memorable statements concerns the delight educated people take in knowing about art, but not knowing about basic electronics or genetics (*AB*, p. 50).

Koestler was an advocate of clean energy, including solar and nuclear power, and among many other things witnessed the demonstration of pioneering instruments such as the electric piano and the electric violin. He marvelled at the magic of science and his love for it was always coupled with a soft spot for mad inventors and a curiosity for its least scientific and most mysterious manifestations. While at Ullstein, Koestler tried to gather reports of occult experiences and was a witness at a particularly unconvincing séance by Eric Jan Hanussen, who, despite his Jewish origins, would later become closely involved with the Nazis. However, the real highlight of his time as science editor came in April 1931 when, on the request of the Ullstein company, Koestler reported on the airship *Graf Zeppelin*'s journey to the Artic. It was at the height of the zeppelin craze and the flight from Germany involved a stop in Leningrad.

Aside from the astonishing views of the landscape below, it meant a lot to Koestler to visit the Soviet Union, for since arriving in Berlin he had been drawn ever closer to the Communist Party. While he had been glad to put Zionist politics and current affairs on hold for the job as science editor, his arrival in Berlin in September 1930 coincided with the first landslide for the National Socialist Party in the Reichstag elections. In this increasingly polarized political climate Koestler was unable to stand on the sidelines.

On the zeppelin voyage via Leningrad, he was overwhelmed by the hospitality of his Russian hosts and thought his utopian hopes confirmed. Walking through the fog back to the airship, Koestler experienced a 'sensation of complete fulfilment' (*AB*, p. 291).

Koestler's road to becoming a Communist did not exclude his Zionism. He was still travelling on a (British Mandate) Palestinian passport and remained a Zionist, as he put it, in a 'limited, resigned and utilitarian sense'.[8] Soviet Communism could in any case be reconciled with the Zionist movement's broader aim to eliminate anti-Semitism, at least as far as its official dogma was concerned.[9] In an increasingly anti-Semitic climate, joining the German Communist Party seemed to him to offer the only convincing response to the spread of Nazi ideas. The Soviet Union itself offered a more audacious utopian vision than Zionist Palestine, one that sold itself as an honest, constructive and unselfish society, in direct contrast to the atmosphere of fear, insecurity, dubious compromise and political hypocrisy that Koestler experienced in Weimar Germany.

The circle of people around Eva Striker, now a former lover, and her current boyfriend, Alexander Weissberg-Cybulski, a Viennese physicist of Polish Jewish origins, played an important role in Koestler's drift towards Communism.[10] Koestler wrote of the importance of two figures in particular who were influential in his conversion: 'Otto' and 'Karl' (*AB*, pp. 233–7). 'Otto' is identifiable as Oto Bihalji-Merin, a Yugoslavian artist and subeditor of the German Communist Party's monthly magazine *Die Linkskurve* (Left Turn), eighteen months older than Koestler. 'Karl', who has never been identified, is given a lively and somewhat unlikely cv in Koestler's autobiography. Koestler describes 'Karl' as a former plumber's apprentice who attended evening classes and made a name for himself as a political writer. He was said to have later written scripts for the Soviet film industry, won a lawsuit against a major Central European company, and tried to sell an invention to Hungarian

entrepreneurs via Koestler's father. After the war, 'Karl' was
living in a country where his Communist past could have proved
problematic. Who was this man? Could it have been Karl Anders
or Kurt Kläber, both former apprentices active in Communist
propaganda in 1930s Berlin? Was 'Karl' living in the USA and at
risk of McCarthy-era repercussions? And could he possibly have
done all these things, or (in light of Koestler's habit of changing
certain details to disguise identities) even similar things?

Like many others, Koestler was profoundly disillusioned
with the German Social Democratic Party, which was thought
to have betrayed its principles and to have unfairly victimized the
Communists. With their charismatic air of mystery and intrigue,
together with their apparent sincerity and loyalty, the Communists
Koestler met seemed to offer a new way of living out his ideals. This
was a time before the cruelty and inhumanity of Stalinist policy in
the 1930s. Koestler steeped himself in the idealistic Soviet Russian
film and literature of the 1920s, which made a deep impact on him,

Reporting on board the *Graf Zeppelin* airship on its journey to the Arctic, 1931.

watching films by Vsevolod Pudovkin and Sergei Eisenstein and reading books by Mikhail Sholokhov, Isaak Babel, Leonid Leonov and Aleksandr Serafimovich. From the perspective of a Jewish Austro-Hungarian 26-year-old living in Berlin, socializing in a clique of dynamic left-wing activists and hangers-on, the Soviet Union truly seemed like a land of promise.

It was at the very end of 1931, around a year and a half after his arrival in Berlin, that Koestler finally decided to join the German Communist Party. With his middle-class background and Revisionist Zionist links, it may seem a surprising step to have taken.[11] Indeed, aside from his understandable opposition to Nazism, he implied that the decision may have also been influenced by losing in a poker game, a dreadful hangover and a broken-down car.[12] He was still the science editor for the *Vossische Zeitung*, but had been given additional responsibilities some months before as the foreign editor of the Berlin daily *B. Z. am Mittag*, and now had a place in editorial meetings for the Ullstein papers.[13] It was an influential position and one which was not tenable with Communist Party membership. In joining the party, Koestler was taking a huge risk with his career, but his position was valuable to the party. He tried to arrange a circle of left-wing sympathizers at Ullstein, but it was not long before his attempts backfired. He was denounced to the management by his assistant, whom he had tried to inculcate, and was required to leave the job. If there was a scandal it was hushed up and the official reason given was the paper's declining sales.

His high-flying career in journalism had suffered a serious setback and, deprived of his comfortable income, he was forced to make new decisions. His Berlin circle was already changing, as Weissberg-Cybulski had left to work as a physicist in Kharkiv, then capital of the Ukrainian Soviet Socialist Republic, and Striker left Berlin in January 1932 to join him. Koestler decided to follow them and arranged a book contract for a title called *Russia through Bourgeois Eyes*. Procuring a visa took several months. Having sent his severance pay from Ullstein to his parents and without a steady job, Koestler tried to earn money by writing fiction. A story he wrote with an old friend and mentor from Budapest, Andor Németh, titled 'Wie ein Mangobaumwunder' (Like a Mango Tree Miracle), was sold to the Munich newspaper the *Münchner Illustrierte Zeitung*. It also brought some interest from the Ufa film studios in Babelsberg, but this came to nothing.[14]

Even before losing his job, Koestler had moved to the so-called 'artists' colony' (*Künstlerkolonie*), a large community housing project for writers and artists, in the Wilmersdorf district of Berlin. There he became part of a Communist cell with Hanns Eisler, Alfred Kantorowicz, Wilhelm Reich and others (Reich and Koestler left subtly different accounts of a fraught night awaiting an attack by the SA).[15] Koestler was at first responsible for propaganda, but his style was soon deemed unorthodox. He remained living in the colony for around six months, until July 1932, when he was able to leave for the Soviet Union. He was becoming inculcated in the culture of the Communist Party, more obsessive in his devotion to the cause, and more able to explain away its hypocrisy and contradictions.

His blindness to any shortcomings of the Communist cause would set him in good stead for the first part of his visit, in which he visited Soviet Ukraine. This was the time of the genocidal Holodomor, the great famine that claimed several million victims in 1932–3. While there was little international awareness of the famine until the following year, Koestler was a witness to it fairly early on. However, unlike his near contemporaries Gareth Jones and Malcolm Muggeridge, who wrote landmark articles for the British press in 1933, Koestler did not immediately publicize his experiences. It was his first encounter with the 'utopia' he had such great hopes for and in his head he explained it all away (*IW*, pp. 50–51). He later wrote that he recognized the hunger in the eyes of those he met and described the terrible scenes he saw and the strategies by which he was shielded from seeing more. According to Koestler, the victims 'choked the railway stations, crammed the freight trains, squatted in the markets and public squares, and died in the streets' (*IW*, p. 56).

In famine-stricken Kharkiv, Koestler stayed with Eva Striker, Alexander Weissberg-Cybulski, and Striker's mother, who was Koestler's old kindergarten teacher. With this strangely familial Communist home as a temporary base, he embarked on an ambitious journey around the Soviet Union to marvel at the achievements of the Five-Year Plan, including the much celebrated Dnieper Dam. He had dual accreditation as a foreign journalist and with the Comintern, which gave him greater freedom than he would otherwise have had. His perspective, though, was that of the enthusiastic convert, not that of an impartial critic. His original account of his travels, including his previous zeppelin trip to the Arctic, *Von weißen Nächten und roten Tagen* (Of White Nights and Red Days), was published in heavily censored form in German in the Soviet Union in 1934. The adventure also forms a significant part of his second autobiography, *The Invisible Writing* (1954).

After the Dnieper Dam, Koestler was due to visit the famine-ravaged Donetsk region as well as German collective farms in Ukraine. These visits were cancelled and so he proceeded to Moscow and from there to the Caucasus and Central Asia. On his travels Koestler met a succession of extraordinary individuals, including a former Russian nun who had been liberated from her convent by the Bolsheviks, a Ukrainian farm worker who had fled her village because of the famine and was travelling to Armenia, a German intelligence officer from Leipzig working in Baku, and a beautiful woman called Nadezhda with whom he spoke in French and fell in love, and whom he also reported to the authorities for stealing a telegram – a betrayal for which he found it hard to forgive himself. From Azerbaijan, Koestler continued to Turkmenistan and Uzbekistan, visiting Bokhara, Samarkand, Tashkent and Ashkhabad, among other places. It was in Ashkhabad that Koestler made the least likely acquaintance of his journey, as his neighbour in the guest rooms of the 'House of Soviets' was the American poet Langston Hughes.[16]

Koestler returned to Moscow and from there to Kharkiv, where he remained for the rest of the winter and spring of 1933, working on his 'Red Days' book in an Intourist hotel room. The famine continued, although as a foreigner Koestler had easy access to food. Food shortages were never mentioned in the local press and nor were the near-permanent power cuts, but even members of the hotel staff were clearly suffering. While Hitler had come to power in Germany and was in the process of dismantling its democratic structures, Koestler was surrounded by a humanitarian catastrophe on a grand scale, about which there was silence throughout the Soviet Union. He attributed this silence to the way information was transmitted in the country, namely by a policy of 'centralisation-plus-atomisation', meaning the centralization of mass media and the discouraging of person-to-person information-sharing. He wrote, 'To understand its full significance, one would have to imagine a world in which travelling is only possible by air, and only due North or due South' (*iw*, p. 152).

Koestler described the absence of reporting on the famine as a surreal experience, but at the time his loyalty did not waver. For the good Communist, it was simply an unfortunate and unavoidable event. It is difficult to understand how educated emigrés living in Ukraine at this time, like Koestler, Striker and Weissberg-Cybulski, were able to rationalize the Holodomor and remain convinced Communists. It came as a great relief to Koestler, however, when the Comintern decided that he should leave the Soviet Union and support their work in Paris. He made a final trip to Moscow where he wrote an unsuccessful film script and made a first sketch of a play, later called *Bar du Soleil*. He also met the major figures whose fates would later inspire his novel *Darkness at Noon*: Karl Radek and Nikolai Bukharin, both Old Bolsheviks who were soon to be purged.

His impression was of men who were spiritually exhausted, mere shadows of their former selves. After Moscow, Koestler travelled back to Kharkiv and from there went by train to Vienna.

Having visited his mother, who was staying with his cousin Margit in Slovakia, Koestler ended up living with his father in Budapest for several months. His friend Andor Németh translated Koestler's play into Hungarian and promised to get it staged, but the production was cancelled because Koestler was a Communist. Nevertheless, through Németh, Koestler was introduced to some of the young stars in the Hungarian literary scene, notably Attila József, whom Koestler deemed Hungary's greatest poet. Koestler started another play, and wrote detective stories with Németh. Internationally, though, tensions were rising. In Austria, Dollfuss had suspended parliamentary government and was attempting to counter the political threat from the National Socialist movement. Pro-National Socialist demonstrations were held in Vienna and Budapest, while anti-Semitic laws were introduced in Germany and the first concentration camps were opened. These events helped quash any misgivings he had about Communism.

Koestler was bound for Paris on Communist Party orders and left Budapest again in September 1933 to take up his job with the renowned propagandist Willi Münzenberg. In Paris he worked with Münzenberg on the second of the 'brown books', published in 1934. The 'brown books' were the German Communist Party's answer to the famous trial which followed the burning of the Reichstag and were seen as a great success. In sharp contrast to his previous jobs, however, Koestler failed to establish himself in Münzenberg's organization and was demoted to organizing anti-Fascist material for the 'German Free Library', which grew out of the research for the 'brown books'. It was during this time that Koestler met his future wife, Dorothee Ascher, the sister-in-law of Koestler's Communist mentor, Oto Bihalj-Merin. Ascher also worked for Münzenberg and Communist politics were at the heart of their relationship.

Koestler left the job in early 1934 and, being hard up financially, pursued other projects. These included co-authoring, on his cousin Ferenc Aldor's request, a reference work about sex titled *L'Encyclopédie de la vie sexuelle*.[17] A return in some ways to his time as a science journalist, it would become his first taste of publishing success. The authors used pseudonyms, though, and Koestler would receive little of the profits. His attempts at fiction continued to flop; an experiment with political fiction for young adults, *Die Erlebnisse des Genossen Piepvogel in der Emigration* (Comrade Dicky-bird's Experiences in Exile), written in German, was derided by the party.

Being better at propaganda than literary prose (at least for the moment), Koestler was soon in charge of publications for the Institute for the Study of Fascism (INFA), secretly funded by the Comintern. Comrade Ivan, as Koestler was known, would work at INFA for the next six months. It was headed by his mentor, Oto Bihalj-Merin. The job was unpaid and Koestler worked for little more than a free lunch. In June he moved to sleep in a hayloft at an alternative community in Meudon-Val-Fleury for a number of weeks, and often walked the two hours to work near the Jardin des Plantes from there. He claimed to have been utterly poor, but very happy, a claim belied only by the fact that, as Iain Hamilton wrote in his biography of Koestler, he had tried to gas himself in a hotel room only a short time before.[18]

Koestler was rescued from vagrancy by Dorothee Ascher. Ascher was a few years younger than Koestler and came from a middle-class family in Berlin. Although far from well off, Ascher had a part-time job and Koestler moved in with her at a run-down hotel on the Île Saint-Louis in the very heart of Paris. Her income, together with the money Koestler made from selling articles to the refugee political magazine *Das Neue Tage-Buch* (The New Diary), was enough to let them get by. He also made friends with the writer Manès Sperber, who had started working at INFA. Soon afterwards, however, internal Communist Party disputes forced both Koestler and Bihalj-Merin to resign from INFA. Combined with increasing insight into the factionalism of left-wing politics, it was the beginning of the end for Koestler's career as a Communist.

Taking the changes in his stride, Koestler began research straight away for the first of his successful novels, *The Gladiators*, which would take another four years to complete. The first distraction from this task came in the form of the Saar status referendum of January 1935, in the run-up to which Koestler was dispatched to the Saar region by the Communist Party to write a satirical weekly paper. The paper was shelved after its first issue, but Koestler was able to publish an article with *Das Neue Tage-Buch* instead. He recognized plenty of the faces in Communist circles in Saarbrücken, many of them familiar to him from Moscow and Berlin.

In January 1935, Koestler and Ascher moved to Zurich to take up an offer of free accommodation there made by Ascher's brother, who was emigrating to the Soviet Union. It was a temporary solution to their housing crisis amid the continuing economic and political uncertainties of the 1930s, which they gratefully accepted. Forbidden contact with the local Party, their life in Zurich was quiet and orderly. Aside from Oto Bihalj-Merin, their friends were mostly Communist or anti-Fascist writers such as Rudolf Jakob Humm, Bernard von Brentano and Julius Hay. And it was in Zurich that Koestler and Ascher got married in June 1935 (not, as Koestler wrote in his autobiography, in March at a joint ceremony with Julius Hay and his wife-to-be, Eva).[19]

Life in genteel Zurich was hard for two down-and-out Communists. Although Ascher loved him deeply, Koestler was incapable of committing to the relationship and demanded she adopt a traditional domestic role, while at the same time he was unable to contemplate a family.[20] Koestler and Ascher separated for several months soon after their wedding. Koestler spent the rest of the year writing a second volume of sexology, *Sexual Anomalies and Perversions*, a rehashing of the work of Magnus Hirschfeld, again on commission from his cousin, and devoted himself to a series of other less successful literary and translation projects. He also continued to publish with *Das Neue Tage-Buch* and work on *The Gladiators*. He was as mobile as ever, moving to Budapest for part of the summer. The Hungarian writer István Vas described meeting Koestler around this time. He did not yet see the talent others seemed to admire and saw him as a 'quivering bundle of nerves whose arrogance was manifestly sustained by his inferiority complex'. Similarly, a friend, Andor Németh, found Koestler quite irritating.[21] After Hungary, Koestler spent several weeks at Lugano in Switzerland living off the generosity of Maria Klöpfer, a wealthy Communist sympathizer interested in Buddhism, who suffered from psychosis. It was an intense, platonic encounter to which Koestler dedicated more space in his autobiography than to his five-year relationship with Ascher, partly because it was an opportunity to question his faith in Marxist ideology and rationalism in general, but also because of its poignancy: Klöpfer was committed to an asylum and died only months later. Communism and the narrative of Western scientific progress were the twin pillars of his rationalist world view, which now 'seemed to give way, as at the slow beginning of a landslide' (*IW*, p. 294).[22]

After Lugano, Koestler returned to Paris and moved in again with Ascher in Montmartre. He continued work on *The Gladiators*, but had to pay his way with other writing assignments. The propaganda chief Münzenberg suggested that he write a satirical sequel with a contemporary political slant to Jaroslav Hašek's *The Good Soldier Švejk* (1923), and with this goal in mind both Ascher and Koestler moved to Bredene, near Ostende in Belgium, for the summer of 1936. There, Koestler and Ascher encountered the novelists Joseph Roth and Irmgard Keun, as well as older acquaintances such as Hanns Eisler and his wife Louise.

However, this Communist literary idyll was not destined to last. The outbreak of the Spanish Civil War provided the thirty-year-old

Koestler, and many other exiles like him, the opportunity to take part in a real Communist crusade. Once again suppressing his doubts about the cause, Koestler hatched a plan with Münzenberg in which he would visit the Franco camp by pretending to be a reporter for the conservative Budapest paper *Pester Lloyd*, where he was still accredited, as well as for the more liberal London-based *News Chronicle*. After a ferry journey from Southampton made tense by the political situation, he travelled via Lisbon to Seville. It was just like his old days as a foreign correspondent. Using speed to his advantage, he obtained an interview with Queipo de Llano, the general who had led the capture of Seville.

However, his stay was to be brief. On the second day, Koestler was recognized by a German journalist whom he had worked with at the Ullstein group, and who knew him to be a Communist. To make matters worse, the journalist was with Nazi airmen. After an unpleasant confrontation which required the intervention of the Nationalist press attaché Captain Bolín, Koestler panicked. He returned to his hotel, packed his suitcase and travelled post-haste to Gibraltar, from where he filed his first story on the Spanish Civil War for the *News Chronicle*.

Koestler spent the next few months in Paris preparing one of the first books on the conflict, a piece of propaganda literature published in German as *Menschenopfer Unerhört* (Untold Victims) and in French as *L'Espagne ensanglantée* (Spain Drenched in Blood). The book included 24 double pages of gruesome photographs of Nationalist atrocities, of which no fewer than thirteen images were of murdered children. It was a crass kind of journalistic truth-telling about which Koestler later felt uncomfortable. He preferred to focus on the contradictions in propaganda, but fighting back aggressively was more the Willi Münzenberg approach (*IW*, p. 334).

After the book's publication, Koestler was sent by the Communist Party (in the guise of Otto Katz's media agency) to report from Málaga in January 1937, although he claimed to be on assignment

for the *News Chronicle*. It took him almost two weeks to travel from
Paris to the war-torn city, accompanied by the Norwegian journalist
Gerda Grepp. A week after his arrival, Málaga was attacked by the
Nationalists. Koestler decided to stay in the city but after four days
the Republicans there were on the brink of defeat. While being
driven from the city with an army colonel, Koestler remembered his
host, Peter Chalmers-Mitchell, a British expatriate and the founder
of Whipsnade Zoo. Out of loyalty he turned back, not knowing
whether it was execution or imprisonment that would await him.
By the following morning, the city had surrendered to Italian
infantry and Spanish soldiers arrived at the Chalmers-Mitchell
villa, among them none other than the press chief from Seville,
Captain Bolín. It had been rumoured that Bolín had ordered
Koestler to be shot and his arrival seemed to indicate the worst.
Koestler was held at gunpoint while soldiers tried to bind his hands
with electrical wire. Frantic negotiation by Chalmers-Mitchell meant
that Koestler's life was spared. He was imprisoned instead.

Menschenopfer Unerhört, augmented with a documentation of
the 102 days the 31-year old Koestler spent in a Spanish jail, led to
the book *Spanish Testament*, published in English by the Left Book
Club in 1937 (the second half of this, which was undoubtedly of
better quality, was later reworked and published as *Dialogue with
Death* in 1942).[23] While the first half of it is extremely partial, the
book is significant not only as a document of the Spanish Civil
War, but as a memoir of prison and of life on death row. The book
describes the psychological pressure of being sentenced to death,
the prisoner's reckoning with it, and the difficulties of creating a
narrative from it. He writes about the people he had the greatest
sympathy for, such as the illiterate peasants condemned to death
for fighting for the right to learn to read. He also comments at
length on prison life and the necessity of having coping strategies.
For him these included things like mathematics, but also keeping
track of time, writing a diary and thinking about abstract topics

such as the future of humanity. For Koestler, mathematics is, as Matthew Taunton has pointed out, a 'mode of writing' which is 'important in articulating political freedom', an association also found in the work of Orwell.[24] For him prison was a surreal and psychologically powerful experience, where perceptions of reality and time were distorted by incarceration. He tried to apply his insights to the way people think in dictatorships, postulating that political inertia can be created by carceral conditions. On leaving jail, Koestler felt that he was never as completely free as he had been there and felt as though he had forgotten his insight into the purpose of suffering. The consciousness, or so Koestler thought, prevents awareness of its own destruction, making even the worst imaginable experience less dreadful in reality. He wrote, 'Nature sees to it that trees do not grow beyond a certain height, not even the trees of suffering' (ST, p. 289).

Reflection on the nature of mortality is another significant part of *Dialogue with Death*. Koestler repeatedly emphasizes that it is fear of dying, not of death, that afflicts those condemned to it. He experiences it when he sees the rows of eyes looking through the spyholes in the prison corridor and when he has flashbacks of the screams of torture heard in the police station in Málaga. At first he is unaware of the number of those killed or of the fact that he has been sentenced to death himself. Later it is his main preoccupation, particularly when he becomes acquainted with the other prisoners and knows when they have been taken to be shot. Death is portrayed as omnipresent, arbitrary, proximate and persistent. As soon as he is aware of the rhythm and practice of killing in the Seville prison, it has a profound psychological effect on him and several times he wakes up shaking in the middle of the night. Death feels at times like something abstract, at times like something immediate and real, at other times irrelevant. These changing thoughts are Koestler's dialogue with death, the fluctuation between feelings of denial, understanding, fear and reassurance.

Franco's troops enter Málaga, 1937. Koestler wrote of his experiences in *Spanish Testament*.

Koestler was rescued from jail by a combination of fluke, powerful friends and a dedicated wife. Peter Chalmers-Mitchell urged the *News Chronicle* to use its influence to save Koestler, which resulted in a concerted international campaign to secure his release. Meanwhile, using Communist Party funds, Dorothee Ascher travelled to London to lobby in person, gaining the support of a number of influential aristocrats and 56 MPs, including Winston Churchill.[25] The public campaign to free Koestler was a success. When Queipo de Llano offered a prisoner swap to Red Cross negotiators in May 1937, Koestler was exchanged for the wife of Carlos Haya, a famous Spanish pilot, who had been taken hostage. Koestler was flown from Seville to La Línea, the Spanish town next to Gibraltar, by none other than Haya himself.

Once in the United Kingdom, there was no romantic reunion with Ascher, although they kept up appearances when required. Ascher had also been campaigning for the cause of her brother

Ernst, who had been arrested in the Soviet Union on spurious charges, but there she was less lucky: he was executed.[26] Koestler began working on *Dialogue with Death* and the preparation of the manuscript for *Spanish Testament*. On its completion in September 1937, Koestler was dispatched by *News Chronicle* to report from Athens and Palestine. He travelled via Paris, meeting Communist Party representatives including Willi Münzenberg, and from there to Zurich, where he paid an awkward visit to Thomas Mann. From Zurich he proceeded to Belgrade, where he was able to meet his parents. Henrik had managed to keep Koestler's imprisonment a secret from Adele until his release from prison. His father was noticeably weakened and it was the last time that Koestler would see him.

Travelling on to Palestine, Koestler found himself alienated from the Zionist cause still further than when he had left the country a decade earlier. As his disillusionment with Communism had increased, so too had his disillusionment with Zionism. If Communism had seemed to him to render Zionism unnecessary,

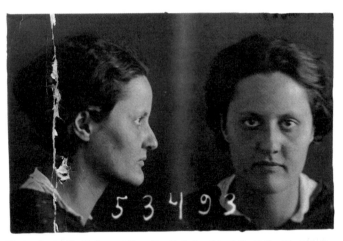

The inspiration for *Darkness at Noon*: Koestler's close friend, Eva Striker (Eva Zeisel) photographed after her arrest in Moscow, 1936.

he now thought of Zionism as an unfortunate necessity, one whose importance was only determined by the persecution of the Jewish people in Europe, as well as the violent resistance to Jewish colonization in Palestine by the Arabs. At this time Palestine was in the midst of a violent revolt against British colonial rule and Jewish settlement and Koestler wrote an article for the *News Chronicle* arguing that partition was the only credible solution.

He returned to London for the launch of *Spanish Testament*, which was selected by the Left Book Club as one of their books of the month and sold over 60,000 copies as a result. Its success gave him the credibility to gain a book deal for his still unfinished novel *The Gladiators* with the publishers Jonathan Cape. His first major success may even become his most enduring, for its sister volume, *Dialogue with Death*, has been said by Louis Menand to have 'a kind of literary permanence that *Darkness at Noon* lacks', in part because of Koestler's decision to depoliticize the book by removing the propaganda elements.[27] Even with them, *Spanish Testament* clearly spoke to the reading public's need to read first-hand accounts of the Spanish conflict. It preceded Orwell's *Homage to Catalonia* (1938), published the following April.

While in London, Koestler met with Eva Striker, his childhood friend and former lover, who had recently been forced to leave the Soviet Union. Both she and her husband had fallen victim to the Stalinist purges and been imprisoned.[28] To make things more complicated, Eva had been having an affair with an NKVD officer named Yakov Ravich-Terzin. She later called him the love of her life, and, having become pregnant, was forced to have an abortion.[29] Of Polish origins, Ravich-Terzin had been a member of the German Communist Party and later worked as Soviet spy.[30] Having been denounced on wholly trumped-up charges (adding Nazi swastikas into her designs and plotting to kill Stalin) by a colleague at the Lomonosov factory where she worked, Eva had spent more than a year in jail, including ten months in solitary confinement, and communicated with her neighbours by knocking on the walls. She had used mind games as a way of maintaining focus, tried playing chess inside her head, while she had heard the screams of those going mad around her. At first resolute not to confess to crimes she had not committed, she eventually signed a confession, which led her to try to commit suicide. Freed by some act of grace, which may have been connected with the arrest of her lover, Ravich-Terzin, Eva was later deported directly to Vienna.[31] Koestler was struck by the parallels to his experiences in Spain and no doubt horrified to hear of the fate of Eva's husband, Alexander Weissberg-Cybulski, who was still imprisoned, as well as that of his own brother-in-law, Ernst Ascher, who died in the purges. His wife Dorothee, too, had suffered from the fallout, losing her job at the German Free Library in Paris.[32]

That his experiences in a Nationalist prison in Spain had been shared by friends and family in the Soviet Union confirmed to Koestler that Communism under Stalin had lost its way. It was not a new realization, however. At a Communist gathering in Spain on his second visit, Koestler had been shocked to hear of the second of the Moscow trials. Later, while in jail, he had told a warder that he was no longer a Communist. It was a telling admission given that his official story was that he never had been one. He had also begun to regret the worst exaggerations in his propaganda work for Münzenberg. He was deeply uncomfortable at the news of Stalinist oppression and made this clear in a speech he gave to an audience of over two hundred German exiles in Saint-Germain-des-Prés in May 1938. Shortly afterwards he resigned from the Communist Party.[33] No longer a Communist, hardly still a Zionist, and with a failed marriage already behind him, the 32-year-old Koestler had come to the end of an exhausting ideological journey. It was the decision that would shape his entire career.

3

Documentarist

The notion of the 'open society', as described by Karl Popper in
The Open Society and its Enemies (1945), describes a form of social
organization in which the individual members are confronted with
decisions, as opposed to the 'closed society' in which the members
are deprived of them, subsumed into a collective mass. Popper's
view was that there can be no 'return' to some imagined utopia
on earth without the consequent destruction of freedom and
humanity.[1] It was an insight, carefully considered and argued,
that Koestler came to himself, not via philosophical reflection,
but by bitter experience.

For Koestler, to become disillusioned with Communism
at precisely the point at which Germany's National Socialist
dictatorship was seeking to expand across Europe must surely
have been a painful process. In resigning from the Communist
Party in April 1938, Koestler had criticized its endemic corruption
and its frequent and unnecessary use of violence against its own
members. He understood that the organization had become
paranoid, inventing 'foreign agents' to legitimize arbitrary crimes.[2]
His break with the party was also the result of a decade of extraordinary personal insights into the failings of Soviet and Socialist
politics both within the USSR and abroad, most notably in Ukraine,
but in Spain as well.

As has been seen, the star journalist Koestler, who possessed
many influential contacts, did not report on the genocidal Ukrainian

famine, even though he had the opportunity to, nor did he give a balanced portrayal of the Spanish Civil War (the first part of *Spanish Testament*, for all the literary qualities of *Dialogue with Death*, remains a one-sided piece of anti-Franco propaganda).[3] Thus his editing of the text for republication in 1942 is emblematic of his conscious shift away from tendentious journalism, presenting pre-drawn conclusions, to a greater honesty in his work and a more reflective and open-ended style of autobiographical and/or fictional literary reportage. His varied contributions are certainly a testament to what has been called the 'elasticity' of the genre, while the ambiguity of his novels vouch for his newfound lack of dogmatism.[4]

From the moment of breaking with Communism to the end of the war, Koestler would associate his name with making amends for his acts of self-censorship in the 1930s by positioning himself as an anti-totalitarian liberal. If his autobiographies are included, this process could be seen as extending right into the 1950s. More often than not, his focus would be on individuals faced with an intellectual dilemma in relation to an encroaching 'closed society' – utopian movements gone wrong.

In the wake of his experiences in Spain, Koestler had been able to secure a book contract in London for his first major novel. Instead of landing in the United Kingdom as an outsider with no contacts in the literary world, as many other exiles did, in some respects, Koestler already had his foot in the door, his first novel also having been published in English translation. In fact, his escape from the Continent came just as his novel *Darkness at Noon* was published, by prior arrangement. In contrast to others, he had a ready-made platform and *Darkness at Noon* is what he did with it.

Koestler's fiction, which had a powerful effect on more than one generation, is not often praised for its aesthetic merits. Rather it is conventionally valued (positively and negatively) for its intellectual content, not least with respect to the politics of the Cold War. In both his memoirs and his novels of the 1930s and '40s, Koestler was able to capture the dilemmas and also the *scenes* of mid-twentieth-century history: the prison cells, yards, night-time operations, streets and encounters where these dilemmas really occurred. Since he was famously poor at describing characters with any depth of feeling, the value of Koestler's fiction, like that of his memoirs, is its documentary quality. This was also a contemporary perception. Writing in *Harper's Magazine* in 1948, the writer and critic V. S. Pritchett disputed that Koestler had written novels at all. In his words, 'They are not novels: they are reports, documentaries, briefs, clinical statements, animated cartoons of a pilgrim's regress from revolution.'[5]

In the decade following his renouncement of Communism, Koestler would develop a trademark mixture of political commentary, reportage and fiction, versions of history that seemed relevant, close to reality, yet without the all-important autobiographical claim to personal experience. It could be argued that his novels are more successful the closer they are to good documentary, based on personal experience of compelling events. This applies within the individual texts as well as across the oeuvre; Koestler's novels are less successful where they revert to 'mere' fiction.

The exception to this rule is, oddly, the first of Koestler's novels, *The Gladiators*, which despite its fairly transparent link to contemporary politics, cannot be said to be a 'documentary novel', still less a work of 'literary reportage'. With the book contract for *The Gladiators* secure, Koestler's first goal after leaving the Communist Party was to complete his novel. Together with *Darkness at Noon*, which was its successor, it would become among the best known of Koestler's fictional works. It is an historical fiction that retells the story of Spartacus's failed revolt against Rome as an early attempt at establishing socialism. It also has a link to Jabotinsky, Koestler's Zionist mentor, who translated Raffaello Giovagnoli's hugely successful 600-page novel *Spartaco* (1874) into Hebrew in 1913.[6] While the Jewish links come through in Koestler's version, it is the allegory of Communism that is its most obvious subject. Koestler's choice of the Spartacus story clearly echoes the name and fate of the failed Spartacus League (*Spartakusbund*) in Germany, of which Rosa Luxemburg and Karl Liebknecht were the most famous members. The League later became part of the German Communist Party, but Luxemburg and Liebknecht were killed following the uprising in January 1919. Unlike its successors, the book did not give much insight into the intellectual dilemma of being a Socialist leader. George Orwell later deemed the book's engagement with the question of revolution unsuccessful, because Koestler did not bring out the ethical dilemma of the revolutionary leader gifted with power.[7]

Despite this perceived failing, it is not a poor book (certainly not by Koestler's inconsistent standards). Pritchett even thought it the best of Koestler's novels.[8] What it dramatizes well is the appeal of Communist utopianism, Communism's pre-Marxian Abrahamic origins (a Koestlerian touch), and its necessary failure. *The Gladiators* coincided with Koestler's loss of faith in the Communist utopia and it is the dashing of naive hopes which is its overall theme.

The Spartacus story has since become ubiquitous, but Koestler's *The Gladiators* preceded the 1951 novel *Spartacus* by Howard Fast which was made famous by Stanley Kubrick's film in 1960. It is even said that the film's producers had originally been keen to adapt Koestler's novel, not Fast's, and that Kubrick wanted to introduce elements of *The Gladiators* into the movie. This was fiercely resisted by the scriptwriter, Dalton Trumbo, for complex political reasons (like both Koestler and Fast, Trumbo was also an ex-Communist).[9]

In Koestler's *The Gladiators*, a group of escaped Roman fighter-slaves from Capua terrorize the Italian countryside and attempt to found an egalitarian state. The utopian political aspects are more clearly present in *The Gladiators* than in Kubrick's *Spartacus* and there is no sentimental love story to rival that between Kirk

Douglas's Spartacus and Jean Simmons's Varinia. The leaders of the group are Spartacus, a fur-clad Thracian, and Crixus, a plodding and uncharismatic Gaul. Their band gains members wherever they roam and soon number in the thousands. They set up camp in the crater of Vesuvius and Spartacus shapes the horde into an army. His idea is that his army will take over a series of towns in Campania and form a 'Sun State'. The inspiration for this utopian society comes from a mysterious, messianic and highly literate masseur with a 'bullet-head', known as 'the Essene'. The Essene is identifiably Jewish and a proto-Communist. His historical notions are nostalgic, based on 'the people's homesickness for the buried times of old that were ruled by justice and kindness' (G, p. 95). Spartacus's success, however, is based on an appeal that the bourgeois townspeople cannot understand. He says to the masses, 'We are the Many and are to serve the Few – why, tell me, why?' (G, p. 119).

Part of the narrative traces the progress of Spartacus and his army; another tells the story from the perspective of the Roman middle classes. The army pillages and burns its way through a series of towns – Nola, Suessula and Calatia – showing no mercy to rich or poor. Spartacus is troubled by his army's brutality but powerless to prevent it. His attempted utopia is marred from the outset by violence. What is more, military success is short-lived. Spartacus and his army are stopped at Capua, where the slaves are duped into defending the city by being granted temporary freedom and weapons.

The rest of the novel documents how the army was split between Crixus and Spartacus, how Crixus's men were defeated by Rome, and how Spartacus made a strategic attempt to realize his 'Sun City' further south near Thurium, in present-day Calabria. Koestler devotes over one hundred pages to the rise and fall of this community, which abjured currencies and hierarchies, and enforced collective labour and living. There are problems from the outset: not all of the newly free citizens consider themselves truly free while they are still obliged to work hard, the methods of discipline are harsh and the establishment of the city does not trigger copycats, as hoped. Restless and greedy, some of the men pillage nearby Metapontum. Another division between Spartacus and Crixus ensues before the experiment is deemed to have failed and Spartacus and his followers vacate and burn the city, setting off for 'home'. There is no home to go to, however, and the ragged army roams Italy before finally being defeated by a Roman army under Crassus. Spartacus is killed, but the book ends with the suggestion of his eventual return. His corpse is said to have disappeared, leaving the future of Spartacus's political ambitions suggestively open (and forming another substantial difference between Koestler and Kubrick's film, in which Spartacus is left dying on a cross).

Having submitted the manuscript, Koestler spent several months helping Willi Münzenberg found the German-language exile journal *Die Zukunft* (The Future) in Paris. Koestler became the journal's first editor. The journal published contributions from a whole array of prominent writers of the day, including Stefan Zweig, Thomas Mann and Sigmund Freud. Koestler even visited Freud in Hampstead to ask him to contribute to the journal (*iw*, pp. 409–10). Koestler did not stay in the job, however, and after *The Gladiators* was published in the spring of 1939, he left *Die Zukunft* to begin work on another book for his cousin, a journalistic hack job about sex and marriage. It was published in English as *The Practice of Sex* in 1939 and the advance for the book meant Koestler had enough money to begin work on his next novel, *Darkness at Noon*.

Koestler's five-year relationship with his wife Dorothee was over, although they were still in contact. Not one to wait around, in Paris in the summer of 1939 and several girlfriends later, Koestler took up with a beautiful English sculptor eleven years his junior. This was Daphne Hardy, the woman who would go on to translate *Darkness at Noon* (and thus create the definitive version of Koestler's text). Hardy had been brought up in the Netherlands, where her father had been involved with the League of Nations court in The Hague. She soon moved in with Koestler in his apartment in rue Dombasle in Paris's fifteenth arrondissement, the same building in which Walter Benjamin was living. In the months before the war, Paris was again full of life. In the words of Janet Flanner, the city experienced 'a fit of prosperity, gaiety, and hospitality' and 'the first good time since the bad time started at Munich'.[10]

Following the Parisian custom of leaving the city for the month of August, Koestler and Hardy travelled together to the South of France. Their first stop was in Roquebrune now Roquebrune-Cap-Martin, sandwiched between Monaco and Menton, near the French–Italian border. Here Koestler began to work on *Darkness at Noon* under the working title 'The Vicious Circle'. Koestler and Hardy then travelled inland to Roquebillière, a mountain village 30 miles to the north. News of the Molotov-Ribbentrop pact of 23 August 1939 reached Koestler while he was still in Roquebillière. It was a devastating turn of events, even for a lapsed Communist, the consequences of which would catch up with him sooner than he imagined.[11] The story of his life over the next couple of years he recorded in his second memoir, *Scum of the Earth*.

Koestler was still in the South of France in early September when he heard that the Second World War had broken out – he was having lunch on the Côte d'Azur with Hardy. In *Scum of the Earth* he describes the idyllic summer of 1939 and the way in which people tried to pretend that the threat was not real. On the brink of war, however, France was in a feverish state of anxiety. Upon returning to Paris from Provence, Koestler was warned that his arrest was imminent, although the grounds were unclear. At first, it seemed as though his decision to leave the Communist Party would have few personal consequences.[12] It has since been revealed that two of Koestler's contacts in the Communist Party, Münzenberg and Katz, were double agents, so Koestler's hunch that he was unfairly denounced by the Communists may be true.[13]

Koestler and Daphne Hardy intended to travel to London, but their decision came just too late: the British authorities cancelled all current visas. Unable to travel amid the general chaos, Koestler was forced to wait a month for his arrest, which finally came on 2 October 1939. After three days spent sitting in a police lecture hall, Koestler and his fellow detainees were taken to the Roland Garros tennis stadium, where a provisional internment camp had been set up. After a week they were transported by train to Toulouse and from there to Le Vernet in the Ariège region. Six weeks after having returned to Paris, Koestler was back in the South of France, this time near the Pyrenees.

By this point, Koestler had been an ex-Communist for a year and a half. The frontmatter of *Scum of the Earth* confirms the certainty of his choice of this position. It begins with an 'Author's Note', in which Koestler states (in as many words) that the German attack on Russia will not alter his critical stance on the Molotov-Ribbentrop pact or the Communist Party in France. The next page is a dedication to a series of German and Austrian writers and journalists who died in the South of France in 1940–41: Walter Benjamin, Carl Einstein, Walter Hasenclever, Otto Pohl and Ernst Weiss. Koestler also includes Irmgard Keun in his list, as Keun was at that time rumoured to be dead. The opening pages of the book therefore see Koestler take up a clear anti-Stalinist and anti-Fascist political and cultural position. He aligns himself with a group of people who were victimized by the Nazi regime and in clear opposition to apologists for Stalin. It was a difficult third way at the time, but one which has been vindicated in hindsight.

Scum of the Earth describes Koestler's experiences in France in 1939 and 1940, including his imprisonment in the notorious camp at Le Vernet. In essence the book is a critique of victimization by bureaucratic power. It is divided into four sections titled 'Agony', 'Purgatory', 'Apocalypse' and 'Aftermath', together with an epilogue. Despite the pathos of the book's title and its chapter titles, Koestler

A satirical drawing from the internment camp at Le Vernet. Koestler documented his experiences there in *Scum of the Earth*.

is wary of aggrandizing his experience and writes that in France in 1939 it was not difficult to find oneself being persecuted. He is also keen to relativize his experiences at Le Vernet, emphasizing how much more humane it was than the German camps. As he put it, 'In Liberal-Centigrade, Vernet was the zero-point of infamy; measured in Dachau-Fahrenheit it was still 32 degrees above' (*SE*, p. 89).

This is no reason to downplay Koestler's experience. In her work on totalitarianism, Hannah Arendt describes the 'atmosphere of madness and unreality' created by the use of concentration camps in the Nazi German and Soviet Russian contexts, a factor which makes it difficult to believe in the authenticity of survivors' experiences and the reality of their existence. Adding nothing to productive capacity, being a drain on economic resources and destroying human capital, the camps only weakened the states to which they belonged. Arendt used similar metaphors to Koestler, dividing concentration camps into three types, 'Hades', 'Purgatory' and 'Hell'. Hades was the run-of-the-mill type of concentration camp like Le Vernet, Purgatory the Russian camps and Hell the Nazi extermination camps. All of them, however, deprived their inmates of their individuality and their place in society and thus of their humanity.[14]

Koestler gives other reasons for the unreality of concentration camp experiences. As in *Spanish Testament*, Koestler describes some of the peculiarities of prison life, such as the persistence of humour in the face of adversity. He describes details of daily routine, camp conditions, the work they were assigned and interactions with fellow inmates. Prison life distorts perspectives, making international events seem smaller and events in the camp seem more important. Several inmates suffer devastating breakdowns; some older men die of ill-health. All the internees obsess about the possibility of their release. Koestler describes prison writing as a genre that is particularly susceptible to dishonesty, to playing down the range of emotions that the prisoner experiences, and playing up suffering. Writers of prison literature are unsettled by their own unexpected resilience, faced with the conundrum that cheerfulness is possible even in inhumane conditions (*SE*, p. 109).

The 'scum of the earth' of Koestler's title were a group of cosmopolitan figures who found themselves on the wrong side of the political authorities in successive countries for one reason or another. They came from Austria, Czechoslovakia, Germany, Spain and elsewhere (*SE*, p. 146). Their wretchedness derived from the way in which they were hounded out, pursued and degraded by this experience. The irony was, of course, that the French government's first move in wartime was to impound those trying to *flee* from the National Socialists. As Koestler points out, some of those interned had effectively been out of work since 1930 and had variously experienced unemployment in Germany, the German concentration camps, the Spanish Civil War, unemployment in France and finally a French concentration camp (*SE*, p. 112). Their internment was also surrounded by secrecy; back in Paris, friends and relatives struggled to find out which authority was responsible for them.

Koestler was released from the camp at Le Vernet on the evening of 17 January 1940, once again largely thanks to considerable behind-the-scenes efforts on the part of his estranged wife Dorothee, and returned to Paris. A new bureaucratic farce ensued, whereby he was required to keep renewing his right to remain in France at irregular intervals. His flat was also again subject to police raids.[15] He compared the situation in France to Kafka's *The Trial*, first published only fifteen years before – a still meaningful literary comparison he would later reuse to describe the Moscow show trials (*se*, p. 150; *iw*, p. 120). As was noted later, there is a certain irony in the fact that Koestler's novel described imprisonment in the Soviet Union, whereas his own experiences of prison were in Franco's Spain and Daladier's France (although the influence of a Communist set-up in the latter episode cannot be excluded).[16] What is more, it was in the period of bureaucratic limbo preceding the military collapse of France that Koestler finished writing *Darkness at Noon*. The translated version was dispatched to London on 1 May. At some point in this period, Koestler submitted a German-language draft of *Darkness at Noon*, under the title 'Rubaschow' (Rubashov), to the publisher Europa-Verlag. Long considered lost, even by Koestler, it was rediscovered by Matthias Wessel in the archives of Zurich Central Library in 2015.[17]

Within days of sending off the manuscript, Koestler was visited by the police and many of his papers were confiscated. Later, he was arrested. Koestler tricked his way out of immediate detention by telling the police he was expected at a government press conference, and went into hiding. He met his wife Dorothee before leaving. Having helped Arthur get out of jail twice, Dorothee was understandably aggrieved that he was intending to flee the country without her.[18] Regardless of this, and through somewhat dubious means, Koestler got himself and Daphne Hardy to Limoges, where he lived under an assumed name and joined the Foreign Legion. In late June 1940, after only a few days spent at the barracks in Périgueux, Koestler deserted from the army and travelled onwards with Hardy to Bergerac, Bayonne and Bordeaux. Bad news awaited them. In Bordeaux, Koestler and Hardy learned that they had missed the last boat to England and that an armistice had been signed between France and Germany. An American journalist offered to drive them to Biarritz, but Koestler was apprehended there by a police patrol and returned to the army barracks in Bayonne while Hardy continued with the journalist towards Spain. Stranded in Bayonne, Koestler sank further into despair. It was in Bayonne that Koestler witnessed the German takeover of the town at first hand. He later described how in that moment he understood why terrorists commit apparently senseless and suicidal acts. In his words, 'I understood that a man could kill to cover his aching nakedness' (*SE*, p. 194).

Together with his fellow soldiers, Koestler left the city and escaped over the demarcation line into non-occupied France. He spent days wandering country roads in the Pyrénées-Atlantiques region in search of the dispersed company, which he finally located in the village of Castetnau-Camblong. He had little reason to celebrate. He believed Hardy to have been drowned in a shipping disaster; he learned that the writer Carl Einstein had committed suicide nearby; and he read that his former mentor Jabotinsky had died in New York. In early August, Koestler finally received orders to demobilize in Marseille, where he fell in by chance with returning former members of the British Expeditionary Force. In their company he was lucky enough to be able to escape. They travelled via the Algerian port of Oran and the Moroccan city of Oujda to Casablanca, and from there on a fishing boat to Lisbon.[19] Two further months of limbo ensued, and Koestler tried to commit suicide using morphine tablets given to him by Walter Benjamin.[20] Finally, Koestler was able to obtain a flight from Lisbon to the UK, although he was immediately arrested on arrival. After several nights in police cells, Koestler spent six weeks in London's Pentonville prison: safe, but not yet free (*IW*, pp. 422–3). After being released in December 1940, Koestler spent the next two months writing *Scum of the Earth*, which was published in 1941.

It is no coincidence that Koestler now saw a unified Europe as the solution to the Continent's political frictions, building on the tradition of Gustav Stresemann and Aristide Briand. In the epilogue to *Scum of the Earth*, Koestler wrote of his belief that only European integration could solve the problem of Germany's expansionist ambitions in the long term (*SE*, p. 253), an internationalist approach being the only way of reconciling ethnic, political and religious diversity with the resilience of nationalist narratives, of making sense of cosmopolitan lives in national contexts. Later, Koestler hoped that the decline of the British Empire and its ruling classes might help the British to Europeanize (*IW*, p. 427). Koestler's analysis of France's collapse in 1940 follows a similar narrative. According to him, France's fundamental failure was its politics of isolationism and its efforts to maintain an outdated national status quo. The Maginot Line – the expensive defensive fortifications built along the German border – was described by Koestler as a symbol of France's 'wish to be left alone' (*SE*, p. 240). Koestler opposed isolationism and supported the war against Germany. However, Koestler's remedy for hatred, which he mentions twice in the book, is not geopolitical. He believed that hatred can only be countered with humour (*SE*, p. 200; p. 255).

Koestler's arrival in Britain coincided with the publication of the novel that would make his reputation, *Darkness at Noon*. One of the ironies of Koestler's political persecution in wartime France was that during the raids on his flat the French police failed to confiscate part of the manuscript of *Darkness at Noon* lying on his desk, itself written and published before *Scum of the Earth*.[21] Koestler had been at work on the novel on and off since the summer of 1939. It is a generational and political novel that dealt with pressing current issues, notably how the Soviet Union should be interpreted and whether 'ends' justify 'means'. The novel recounts the trial of a fictional old Bolshevik named 'Nicolas Salmanovitch Rubashov', a figure intended as a composite of Nikolai Bukharin, Leon Trotsky and Karl Radek, although at least part of the inspiration for the novel drew on Eva's experiences (she did not read the novel for forty years after its publication, the memories being 'too painful').[22] And while it cannot be described as a work of autobiographical fiction, it does contain fictional elements that draw on the author's personal experiences (*IW*, pp. 386–7; pp. 394–5). It is structured in four parts, corresponding to the three hearings of Rubashov's trial and a retrospective summing-up after judgement has been passed. It opens with Rubashov's arrest and closes with his execution. It is a novel of ideas written for a general audience and despite the seriousness of its subject matter and its political intent, its style is intended to be witty and accessible. It was originally written in German but was first published in English translation.

Writing fiction enabled Koestler to reflect philosophically on his decision to reject the Communist Party in an accessible way. In Iain Hamilton's words, *Darkness at Noon* was 'a fearful revelation of the nightmarish realities of Communism in practice', while for David Cesarani it was the beginning of the 'final rout' which led to the collapse of Soviet Communism in 1989–90.[23] V. S. Pritchett termed it a 'tour de force', but one limited by melodramatic qualities.[24] The book wears its anti-Communism on its sleeve and makes little secret of the fact that it is set in a fictionalized Russia and is essentially an imaginary retelling of the Moscow show trials in the 1930s – deeply divisive events which split the European left. It is also notable that the novel, which was published midway through the Second World War, references the 1930s famine in Russia and Ukraine (*DN*, p. 158). *Darkness at Noon* is a generational novel both in the sense that it responded to an ethical crisis experienced by a particular mid-twentieth-century generation caught between Stalin and Hitler, and also in a limited, literary-historical sense in that it presents an intergenerational conflict with only male characters and diagnoses a crisis of 'cultural inheritance'.[25] Rubashov, a famous party member and a protagonist of the revolution, belongs to the older generation. Initially his interrogation is conducted by one of his contemporaries, Ivanov, but soon a new, younger interrogator replaces him. Gletkin, as the man is named, is both Rubashov's legacy and his nemesis. He was only a boy at the time of the revolution and came of age during the Civil War. Unlike the men of Rubashov's generation, he has no ties to the pre-revolutionary world (*DN*, pp. 185–7).

The relevance of the questions raised in *Darkness at Noon* have been said to extend beyond their twentieth-century context. Even in 1942, the critic Malcolm Cowley suggested that its theme of political morality was an eternal one.[26] The same can be said of the discourse on history in *Darkness at Noon*, which is particularly striking. It contrasts linear and circular conceptions of time, as well as relativist and objectivist notions of historical truth. Rubashov's generation naively thought that history could be conducted as an experiment that it was possible to repeat. Only the loss of human capital taught them the impossibility of experimenting with the future (*DN*, p. 160). On the other hand, Rubashov also perceives a historical 'pendulum movement' in the amount of political freedom a society enjoys, swinging backwards and forwards between democracy and autocracy, from which it is difficult, if not impossible, to escape. Similarly, Rubashov is critical of the attempts by the younger generation to rewrite history. However, what Rubashov perceives as revisionism is also at odds with Gletkin's generation's belief that a day will come when it is finally safe to open the archives, when the necessity and importance of the show trials will be demonstrated to the world (some manipulation of the evidence notwithstanding) (*DN*, p. 117;

p. 159). Rubashov is tormented by this notion that the party represents historical destiny and the possibility that the morally dubious actions of 'No. 1' (as the Stalin figure is dubbed in the novel) might ultimately be vindicated, even though he had formerly defended this view himself (*DN*, pp. 43–4). Gletkin, meanwhile, has few qualms about the ethics of narrating complicated or difficult moments in history. He believes that the 'masses' are only capable of understanding repeated, simplified, exaggerated and unambiguous propaganda messages (*DN*, p. 226; p. 234).

Tony Judt insists it is not a book about Communism or those whose lives it blighted, but rather about Communists.[27] As a predecessor to Orwell's *1984* (1949), the book's depiction of a clash of mindsets had a lasting influence on Soviet Studies in the West. Today Koestler's paradigm can be seen as potentially limiting, but at the time it was seen as the archetypal representation of the threat posed by Communism to the liberal, free-thinking subject.[28] The main thrust of the novel concerns the 'ends and means' debate, which is not as simple as the intergenerational conflict might superficially imply. Rubashov may belong to the older generation, but he is still a Bolshevik. He believes the revolution's success was to enlist Machiavellianism in the service of 'universal reason', rather than 'national romanticism' (*DN*, p. 98). Gletkin, however, accuses Rubashov of sharing the political views of a delegation of women from Manchester, who were shocked by how much worse the conditions for workers were in the Soviet Union as compared to Great Britain. Gletkin sees their arguments as ahistorical as they forget that at the beginning of the Industrial Revolution, workers' conditions in Britain were also extremely poor. The women from Manchester protest the means of industrial progress, but neglect to consider both beginnings and ends (*DN*, p. 225). Gletkin does not find it easy to convince his opponent. In the third hearing, Rubashov makes a barbed, satirical confession of his political wrongdoings, saying, 'I have lent my ear to the laments of the sacrificed, and thus become deaf to the arguments which proved the necessity to sacrifice them' (*DN*, pp. 189–90).

Roger Berkowitz has compared Koestler's concerns to those of Hannah Arendt in *The Human Condition* (1958), suggesting that the book's central question concerns the 'political importance of decency'.[29] Confronted with the possibility of his death, Rubashov is able to give up the forced objectivity and materialism of the party line. He experiences a mystical feeling of infinitude, much like the one Koestler described experiencing as a boy in Budapest. These feelings become real to him for the first time, despite the party's official disapproval of such notions. He realizes that this 'oceanic' sense of wonder at the absolute is his true heresy (*DN*, p. 257). Just before the end of the book, the thought occurs to Rubashov that the current teleological understanding of 'economic fatality' might in the future be combined with this sense of wonder. If so, the means of political action might finally be forced to justify the ends and a humanitarian approach might prevail. It seems that Rubashov agreed with the women from Manchester after all. It is also important to note that the wrongs of the political system are not ultimately seen by Rubashov as unique to Communism. *Darkness at Noon* is an anti-totalitarian novel, as much as an anti-Communist one, despite the specificity of its critique.

Instead of facing the death sentence like his character Rubashov, Koestler's final time behind bars (at least for political reasons) ended in his release. Koestler was reunited with Daphne Hardy at Pentonville Prison while still in custody. Several things had happened in the time that he had been off-radar. In Koestler's absence Hardy had had the distinction of giving *Darkness at Noon* its English title, inspired by Job 5:14.[30] Koestler also learned of his father's death in July 1940 from complications following a cancer operation at the Jewish Hospital in Budapest.[31] Koestler wrote later that both his parents feared that he had fallen into Nazi hands. The day before he died, his father had allegedly asked for Arthur's photo to be removed from the bedside, telling Adele, 'I can bear it no longer' (*IW*, p. 376).

Around Christmastime in 1940, Koestler and Hardy moved in together in a house near South Kensington underground station and Koestler began work on *Scum of the Earth*. They did not live there together for long, though, as Koestler signed up for the Pioneer Corps of the British Army, a unit open to foreign nationals and older men which undertook support tasks within the UK. From April 1941, he served in Ilfracombe and Avonmouth and was recruited by the Army Educational Corps to give lectures to troops. Meanwhile, *Scum of the Earth* was published and received particularly glowing reviews in the American press.[32]

Koestler's educational and literary activities put him on a collision course with the Pioneer Corps. He may have faked a nervous breakdown to obtain a transfer to the Ministry of Information in London and he was discharged from the army in March 1942. Moving to the capital, Koestler was propelled into the inner circles of the London literary scene. He exchanged letters with E. M. Forster, had tea with George Orwell and drank with Dylan Thomas.[33] Not having anywhere to live, Koestler moved into a shared flat with the *Horizon* editor Cyril Connolly, but eventually Koestler proved to be too fussy a flatmate. When Hardy was also given a position at the Ministry of Information, Koestler moved in with her in a cottage in Chelsea, just off King's Road.

Koestler was now 36 and with four books behind him was established as a literary name. He wrote a column for the *Evening Standard* and was involved in pieces of political propaganda such as his film script 'Lift Your Head, Comrade', filmed by the Documentary Film Unit, as well as radio plays for the BBC Home Service and German Service.[34] His English hosts made fun of his 'harsh' accent but there were various clues that he was under more serious emotional pressure elsewhere in his life. The experience of years of activism, high-stakes journalism and political persecution had made him into a heavy drinker who was aggressive in debate, touchy and patronizing. He had better moments, though, and could be charming and confident. Whether through his humour, his persistence or his growing fame, Koestler still attracted considerable attention from women.[35]

Hardy put up with Koestler's infidelity and his bad moods for a while yet. While living with Hardy in Chelsea, Koestler wrote his third novel, *Arrival and Departure*, focusing on the personal crisis of an intellectual on the run from Nazism and trapped in a neutral country. The book was based on Koestler's experiences in Lisbon and is considered one of the first novels to talk about the Holocaust. A year of domesticity passed, which Koestler also spent writing articles and giving talks and lectures, but Koestler was keen to put an end to it. When in the autumn of 1943 he was invited to move to two rooms in George Strauss's mansion in Kensington Palace Gardens, he gladly accepted. Strauss was of a similar age to Koestler and was at that time the Labour MP for Lambeth North.[36]

On its publication in November 1943, *Arrival and Departure* was met with a mostly sceptical response. Orwell thought it dealt only superficially with the question of the limitations of socialist revolution, an exacerbation of the same problem which Orwell had detected in *Darkness at Noon* as well as *The Gladiators*.[37] V. S. Pritchett thought it 'rotten'.[38] Yet it was undoubtedly timely. Only a year before, a joint Allied declaration read in the House of Commons on 17 December 1942 gave credence to reports that the German government had enacted Hitler's plans to exterminate the Jews of Europe en masse. The official text declared that the 'number of victims of these bloody cruelties is reckoned in many hundreds of thousands of entirely innocent men, women and children', but this proved to be a drastic understatement.[39]

A chapter from *Arrival and Departure* published in the October 1943 issue of *Horizon* had been met with scepticism by many readers due to its portrayal of Nazi mass killings.[40] In an otherwise patchy novel, the eleven or so pages describing the night-time transport by train of Jews, Roma and political prisoners are undoubtedly among the most compelling. The novel's hero, an ex-Communist called Peter Slavek, is a non-Jewish survivor of the transport and a witness to the terrible conditions in the trains, the division of the prisoners by category, of the panicked reactions of some and the attempts to maintain dignity by others. Those Jews deemed useless are gassed in specially adapted train carriages, while those left alive chant 'How shall we feast when the Messiah arrives' (*AD*, pp. 86–97). The effect is chilling.

Perhaps the Commons declaration had only confirmed Koestler's worst fears. His despair revealed itself in bouts of heavy drinking, aggression, remorse and repeated breakdowns. It also spurred him into political engagement. Koestler had already renewed his interest in Zionism, meeting Chaim Weizmann in 1943, but now took to attending the Palestine Luncheon Club as well as meetings of the Anglo-Palestine Committee. When Hungary was occupied by Nazi Germany in March 1944, Koestler feared that his mother would be killed, particularly as he heard that several members of his Jewish family had been deported.[41] It is difficult to imagine the personal cost to Koestler and many others like him of the wave of political terror that had swept Europe since the early 1930s. Many of his friends from Communist days, including his brother-in-law Eric, had been killed in the USSR; others, such as 'Paula' and Ernst Schneller, died in Nazi prisons. His old Austrian journalist friend Bruno Heilig was imprisoned in Dachau, while his Aunt Rosa, his cousin Margit and her two children were all killed at Auschwitz. Two of his Berlin girlfriends were killed in concentration camps, two others in air raids. His one-time mentor Willi Münzenberg had committed suicide near Grenoble, his Paris neighbour Walter Benjamin had killed himself at the Spanish border, and his Uncle Otto had committed suicide in Berlin in 1942.

This short list of personal loss is only a snapshot of the many people in Koestler's life who did not survive Stalinism or Nazism. Throughout the war, Koestler attempted to raise the profile of the victims of Nazism through the means at his disposal as a writer: letters, lobbying and financial aid.[42] In his autobiography, Koestler wrote of his fury at the refusal of many British people to take the Holocaust seriously in 1943, which had affected the reception of *Arrival and Departure* (*IW*, pp. 428–9). It would be interesting to speculate what, if any, insight Koestler had into the government control of information about the Holocaust from his work with the Ministry of Information. As Michael Fleming has demonstrated, the genocidal purpose of Auschwitz could have been publicized from November 1942 onwards, but it seems that the British government was reluctant to do so. It was not until July 1944 that credence was really lent by media outlets to the numerous rumours

Koestler's Hungarian passport, 1940s.

and reports about Auschwitz.[43] Only weeks later, the first Nazi extermination camp was liberated by Soviet forces at Majdanek, near Lublin, Poland.

In the midst of his depression, Koestler's relationship with Daphne Hardy was also falling apart. He had been pursuing another woman, Mamaine Paget, since he met her at a party hosted by Cyril Connolly in January 1944. Mamaine and Celia Paget were twins, well-connected society girls who had been orphaned at a young age.[44] Koestler's relationship with Mamaine grew over the spring and summer of 1944, despite his attempts to put an end to it – he felt it was inappropriate given the political situation in Europe. Meanwhile, circumstances with Daphne deteriorated still further and she finally left him in May. Like his wife Dorothee before her, Daphne felt poorly served for all her support of Arthur since 1939. When she visited him more than a year later, she was still bitter about his treatment of her.[45]

Koestler began to recover from his depression in June 1944, possibly with medical help, around the time of the Normandy landings. Following the liberation of Paris in August 1944, Koestler was further heartened to hear that his wife Dorothee had survived the occupation in hiding. His mother, too, was still alive, but struggling to survive amid challenging circumstances in Budapest. She even lived in the city's ghetto for a time, before the city was liberated by the Red Army in February 1945.[46]

Amid the chaos that surrounded him, Koestler decided to return to Palestine. Assisted by Chaim Weizmann, who hoped Koestler might help persuade the Zionist Revisionists of the merits of partition, he was able to travel there by boat, embarking in late December 1944 and arriving in Jerusalem in January 1945. In the half-year he was in Palestine, Koestler spent two weeks doing research for a new novel at the Ein Hashophet kibbutz and took part in a night-time operation to establish a new settlement on the tower-and-stockade model. He also spent time in Arab villages, trying to see the situation from their perspective.[47] Otherwise, Koestler spent his time in Jerusalem beginning work on a novel about Zionism, *Thieves in the Night*, and writing articles for the British press.

The war in Europe ended while Koestler was still in Palestine, so he missed the celebrations in London, but returned there on 12 August 1945, just a few days before the declaration of victory over Japan. This means that he heard the news of the atom bomb dropped on Hiroshima on 6 August while still in Palestine. He would later describe this date as the most important in the history of mankind (*J*, p. 1), because it symbolized the technological possibility of rapid man-made human extinction.

Koestler's relationship with Mamaine Paget was non-exclusive during his time in Palestine, and although he planned to live with Paget on his return to the United Kingdom, Koestler also had an affair with a woman named Anny Bauer. Bauer became pregnant by Koestler, but had an abortion. On his return, Koestler and Paget moved in together in a house in Snowdonia in North Wales. Koestler continued to work on his novel but relations with Paget became strained in 1946 as he tried to delegate secretarial tasks to her, essentially enforcing the traditional gender roles that had marred his relationship with his wife, Dorothee.[48] In Wales, they were visited by George Orwell, as well as by Paget's sister Celia and Koestler's still-aggrieved ex-girlfriend Daphne Hardy.

In a landmark essay titled 'The Yogi and the Commissar', which was published in *Horizon* magazine in June 1942, Koestler elaborated on his discourse on ends and means. He believed that the essay dealt with the fallacy that oppressive measures such as the planned socialist economy could lead to a 'free and happy' society (*IW*, p. 389). His starting point was once again the perceived opposition of Stalinism and Nazism, but in the essay he sought to sketch out a general theory of ideological difference. He conceived of a political spectrum that ranged from the infrared to the ultraviolet, with the 'Commissar' and the 'Yogi' representing the respective sides. The Commissar believes that the ends justify the means, while the Yogi believes that only the means are important. In between the two extremes, compromises are possible. However, Koestler argued that there was a mutual lack of comprehension between political opinion at the two extremes, that the two cannot account for each other using their respective theories, and that despite thinking themselves to be mutually exclusive, they are in fact interdependent.

Koestler thought the failure of revolutionary actions were due to two intellectual contradictions, the 'Antinomy of the Serpentine' and the 'Antinomy of the Slopes' (*YC*, p. 17). The first refers to the way revolutions burn out. As the forces of the revolution travel up a winding mountain road towards utopia, they have the tendency to oust their leader and then follow him over the cliff. The second refers to the necessary consequences of making compromises on the ways in which the revolution's goals are to be achieved, the 'half-way houses' built on the slopes of the utopian mountain. As soon as you believe that the ends can justify the means, you begin to slide down the mountain and eventually achieve the opposite of your intended goal. In this context, he quoted Blaise Pascal: 'he who would act the angel acts the brute.'[49]

He argued that the interdependency of the Commissar's and the Yogi's ways of thinking was echoed by the necessity in physics to take account of metaphysics, or the importance of the irrational instincts of the masses in a socialist's explanations of the continued failure of their cause. Similarly, the Commissar does not allow for thinking about life after death, but by virtue of his tendency towards violence is destined to meet his end sooner rather than later. Koestler likened the revolutionary to a permanent adolescent, trapped in an existential crisis and failing to deal with the absolute (*YC*, p. 20). He also thought that disillusioned, disappointed socialists suffering from a 'pink hangover' were predisposed to envy the Fascists, rather than to hate them, and thought this might lead the one to imitate the other's methods (*YC*, p. 22).

In 'The Yogi and the Commissar' Koestler repeated the notion of the pendulum motion within history touched upon in *Darkness at Noon*, the idea that progress will always be met with reaction. Later, in the companion essay 'The Yogi and the Commissar (II)', written in 1944, Koestler extended this binary into the domain of knowledge, contrasting exploration and contemplation as two complementary epistemologies (*YC*, pp. 222–3). In the 1942 essay, though, using the metaphor of the tide flowing upriver in an estuary, Koestler indicates that reaction does not ultimately hinder progress, but that knowledge of progress is necessary before one can understand the often destructive responses to it. In this alternation between the infrared and ultraviolet modes, it is as if humanity enters periods of dream or nightmare, which are contrasted with a prosaic and sometimes brutal reality (*YC*, p. 25).

Calling Koestler an anti-Communist brings out his opposition to Stalinism, but masks his sincere interest in utopian communities, their success and their failure. In *The Gladiators* the uneasy balance between idealism and mercenary opportunism leads to the failure of the Spartacus uprising, while in *Thieves in the Night* the Zionist kibbutz movement is shown as well-organized but is also plagued by infighting. Similarly, focusing on the 'ends and means' debate, which features in *Darkness at Noon* as well as in his essay 'The Yogi and the Commissar', distracts from another continuity, Koestler's documentation of the abuse of power and the psychological worlds of incarceration and political persecution in *Scum of the Earth* and *Darkness at Noon*, which in a literary sense also build on his earlier work *Spanish Testament* (or *Dialogue with Death*).

Koestler's major relationship between 1938 and 1944 was with Daphne Hardy, although he maintained sporadic contact with his wife Dorothee. Partly with Hardy's help, and later with Paget's, Koestler completed a series of novels and his second memoir, which contain ideas about contemporary political realities that were legitimated by his own experiences as a writer, journalist and political activist. Koestler was personally affected by the Holocaust, but also by the Stalinist purges, culminating in a personal crisis towards the end of the war. Koestler responded with a renewed engagement with the Zionist cause, but again did not remain in Palestine and returned instead to England.

4

Infamy and Autobiography

It is roughly at this point, if not before, that the 'hatchet job' biography on Koestler could kick in, for his personal and professional successes were succeeded by as many lows. Following the success of *Darkness at Noon*, which sold well in the years immediately after the war, Koestler was handed a valuable opportunity, but the opportunity was also a sort of trap. As well as financial stability, fame and success brought danger – there was always a potential risk of belated reprisals for his political interventions of the 1940s. Koestler had an intercom installed at his London home and allegedly kept a gun in his bedroom, while George Steiner said that Koestler was probably number three on the Soviet hit list.[1] Koestler also faced the nearly impossible task of maintaining his reputation as a prominent dissident literary voice.

Without any new cause to rival his political experiences of the 1920s and '30s, Koestler did not produce further novels of the intensity of *Darkness at Noon* or *Thieves in the Night*. Later successors on the best-seller lists like Harper Lee or J. D. Salinger solved this problem by avoiding public life, but Koestler was different. In contemporary debates on the political role of literature, he had already taken sides.[2] At first he chose to continue with his signature mixture of political activism, novel writing and autobiography, but eventually he turned to older interests in science and philosophy.

Today, the post-war period in Britain is seen as a time of rebuilding, with the creation of the NHS and the modern welfare state. It was also a time of ongoing military engagement, continued rationing and national service. More than any other period, it is seen as a time of transformation, of redefinition, and then, as the new status quo became accepted, of increasing social conformity. For Koestler, the major issue at hand was the future of British Mandate Palestine, a potential place of refuge that had been forbidden to many European Jews. While he was voicing public concern about Stalinism, Koestler was also actively supporting the Zionist movement. This position, which today might seem closer to the politics of American Republicanism, brought him into the political and intellectual circles of the Labour Party. Working with the MPs Richard Crossman and Michael Foot, Koestler helped draft a pamphlet titled *A Palestine Munich?* (1946). It argued that Chamberlain's 1939 White Paper on Palestine was, like Chamberlain's policy of appeasement of Hitler, a failure, and that it sold out on the needs of thousands of European Jewish refugees and capitulated to the demands of the Arabs (it permitted only 75,000 Jewish refugees to settle in Palestine). The pamphlet advocated the creation of a Jewish state with no immigration quotas, and the ceding of the larger West Bank area to Jordan (then called Transjordan), with Palestinian Arabs being granted Jordanian citizenship.[3] It was a new departure in Labour policy, which had hitherto backed a single-state solution in Palestine.

Koestler saw Palestine's future as one of the defining issues for the British Empire's legacy in international affairs. In an article for the *New Statesman* in 1947, Koestler argued that as a declining power, Britain should see its moral integrity as linked to the future of the Palestine question. He wrote of his own family's fate under the Nazis and pointed out that many Jewish terrorists had similar backgrounds. He again criticized the actions of the British in 1939, writing that 'at the very moment when the extermination of the European Jews began, the doors of Palestine were slammed in their faces.'[4]

This radical pronouncement, undoubtedly still shocking to a British ear, continued the tone of the novel that ensued from Koestler's second stint in Mandate Palestine, *Thieves in the Night: Chronicle of an Experiment*, which was published in 1946, two years before the establishment of Israel as a state. The novel is set in the years leading up to the Second World War, and is a fictionalized account of the foundation of a kibbutz-type communal farm in Mandate Palestine by a group of European Zionists. Written against the background of the Nazi persecution of Jews in Europe, the novel portrays the intensity of commune life, the challenge of formulating a Jewish identity in the process of profound change, and the moral and political dilemmas of the Zionist cause. It is fiercely critical of the prevention of Jewish immigration into Palestine by the British colonial authorities at the height of Hitler's power in Europe and shows how this perceived inhumanity radicalizes the educated protagonist Joseph, who is half-Jewish and from England, and leads him into organized terrorism.

As in Koestler's previous books, fictional and autobiographical, the novel makes extensive use of diary entries as a narrative device as well as of interior monologues. Following what has become a popular critique of Koestler, Edmund Wilson disputed that the work was a novel, instead praising it for its journalistic merit.[5] At the heart of the novel is a set of tensions that encapsulate a pioneer's experience in Palestine in the interwar period and in the shadow of Nazism. These include the impact of anti-Semitic political (and possibly also sexual) violence on personal relationships, as seen in the story of the book's most tragic figure, Dina. Although Dina and Joseph fall in love with one another, Dina cannot bear to be touched by a man. Meanwhile, the idealistic aspect of Zionism is portrayed in the specific context of the socialist kibbutz movement. This idealism is shown to be idiosyncratic and frequently conflicted, not least in its love–hate relationship towards the Soviet Union, but the kibbutzniks are mostly portrayed in a sympathetic manner. Above all, the novel discusses the tensions between the Zionist settlers, the Palestinian inhabitants and the British colonial authorities. It does so with success and contemporary reviews judged it one of the best of Koestler's works, although it was, like his other books (in Isaac Rosenfeld's words), 'a dramatized problem'.[6]

The book conveys the settlers' idealistic, utopian mood. It opens with a stealthy night-time operation to establish a new commune, called Ezra's Tower. A forty-strong militia, followed by the designated group of settlers, transport a prefabricated watchtower on a truck with dimmed headlights, set it up at sunrise and begin to construct a stockade and the first huts. The wall and tower method was an early symbol of Jewish settlement in Palestine, being exhibited at the 1937 World Exposition in Paris, and has been said to 'transform the landscape into a battlefield' and lend it an urban character.[7] In the novel, the land occupied is legally acquired by the National Fund and is lying fallow, perhaps even since the last 'Hebrews' left the area more than a thousand years before. The settlers are thus shown creating an oasis in the wilderness. It is a process that has moments of joy and elation, but just as often the atmosphere is nervous and fraught. The future of Jewish immigration to Palestine and the possible partition of the country are the political questions that are foremost in the characters' minds, but they also have more pragmatic concerns, such as how to thwart violent attacks from resentful Palestinian locals.

As can be deduced from this, the Arab figures in the book are much less flatteringly depicted. A local village chief, the Mukhtar of Kfar Tabiyeh, is an ingratiating and divisive figure, while his moody son, Issa, is known to be responsible for the attempted rape and brutal murder of Dina. The Palestinian Arabs are said to be lazy and poorly organized; they suffer from preventable diseases and have not caught up with modern agricultural methods. The novel is frequently critical of the Zionist pioneers and the reality of the commune, but it also privileges their voices, values and

Koestler at Kibbutz 'Hagarin' in Mandate Palestine, March 1945.

aspirations. The pioneers were victims of injustice, particularly due to the hapless policy of the British administration. As Koestler writes in the novel, 'The wooden plough had to be protected against the noisy tractor, the thirsty earth against the artifice of irrigation . . . For behold, there was still justice in the world which looked after the feeble' (*TN*, p. 226).

While the first two parts of the book describe the establishment of the commune, its daily life and the tensions with the neighbouring Arab village, the third section of the book portrays Joseph's turn towards terrorist violence. His motivations are political as well as personal. Dina, a woman he loved, has been murdered, and he is also passionately opposed to the British administration's increasingly restrictive immigration policy. In Haifa, Joseph witnesses the stand-off between port officials and a refugee ship prevented from landing, and attends the immigration trial of a German-speaking Jew who had escaped from Dachau concentration camp and entered Palestine illegally. He makes contact with friends in the paramilitary group Irgun, which historically was connected with Koestler's former friend and mentor Jabotinsky. He assists the Irgun in smuggling in refugees stranded on a boat, and agrees to do propaganda work for them. A few days later, Zionist protestors run riot at local government buildings in Tel Aviv and destroy the list of illegal immigrants.

Koestler wrote one of the very first pro-partition articles in the leading British daily, *The Times*, and later claimed that members of the 1947 United Nations Commission which endorsed the creation of Israel had read his novel and that he was proud of its role in influencing them.[8] However, in today's climate, when the Israel–Palestine issue is still one of the most important stumbling blocks in international politics, the book cannot simply be celebrated. In his influential polemic *The Question of Palestine* (1980), Edward Said mounted a critique of biased portrayals of Israel and Palestine. He outlines the 'denial' and subsequent 'diffusion' of the problems faced by the Palestinian people, claiming that Palestinians have been denied a voice and have been poorly served in representations of the Israel–Palestine conflict.[9]

Koestler's *Thieves in the Night* provides evidence for some of Said's claims but belies others. Contrary to how Said characterizes Zionist representations of Palestine and of kibbutz-type farms in particular, the novel portrays Palestine as inhabited predominantly by Arabs, dramatizes disputes over the ownership of land and does not neglect to include the Arabs' perspective on the Jewish settlers.[10] Furthermore, while Said unquestioningly repeats the nationalist assumption that peoples have a natural 'bond' to geographical locales, Koestler contrasts diasporic Jewish identities with their no-longer-imagined home, takes note of the centuries of Palestinian history and sees the Palestine-born children of Zionist Jews as representing a break with their own heritage, not the continuation of it.[11] However, where Said's critique is pertinent to *Thieves in the Night* is in the book's reproduction of broader negative narratives on Palestinian Arab culture and its implicit claim that the moral superiority of Zionism was augmented by the brutality of the Holocaust, as well as in the othering of Palestinian Arabs by Zionist commentators posing as 'expert Orientalists' who presumed to speak in their name (Koestler being one of them).[12]

At the time, however, the most controversial aspect of *Thieves in the Night* and *Promise and Fulfilment* was Koestler's apparent support of Jewish paramilitary violence. Aside from allegations that Koestler was writing in support of terrorism, the other issue that accompanied Koestler through the mid- to late 1940s was the belated aftermath of his novel *Darkness at Noon*. Although the book sold poorly at first in Britain, it received a book club endorsement in the United States, where it enjoyed solid sales and secured Koestler's income. The book was successful in France, too, where readers queued up to buy it and booksellers refused to sell it. *Le zéro et l'infini*, as it was called in French, sold in excess of 300,000 copies in the period 1945–8 and initiated an exemplary case of 'reading as a public exercise in reasoning'.[13] *Darkness at Noon* also prompted a critique by the philosopher Maurice Merleau-Ponty, titled *Humanism and Terror*, which attacked Koestler's ideas (and, according to some readers, also disagreed with itself).[14] Merleau-Ponty's analysis of Koestler rests on the assumption that

Koestler was trying to criticize Marxism from within without fully understanding it. His summaries of the questions posed by *Darkness at Noon* are broadly correct, but the attempted steamrollering of Koestler's credibility falls flat, because Merleau-Ponty does not allow for the fact that he and Koestler are singing from different hymn sheets. Koestler had already abandoned Marxism-Leninism; Merleau-Ponty was still clinging on.[15]

Koestler was at the height of his notoriety in France and living in North Wales when his mother arrived from Hungary in July of 1946. She was two weeks late, and, having waited around in London for her, Koestler had already returned to Wales. He came back to London to meet her, but left again after spending only three days in her company. Adele was then sent off to Surrey. Koestler had secured a place in a nursing home for Jewish refugees in Ashtead, which was run by someone Adele knew. Adele was not terribly happy at the prospect of moving to the Home Counties. She was still a long way from her son, and she did not have many friends and members of her family left following Nazism, the Holocaust and the war. Moving to England promised security, but also a new kind of social isolation.[16] Koestler was keen to avoid too much contact.

In October 1946, almost eighteen months after the end of the war, Koestler returned to Paris for the first time. One surprise was that some of his furniture and even a draft of *Darkness at Noon* had survived in his flat there. His play *Twilight Bar* was being staged by Jean Vilar, who would go on to found the renowned Avignon Festival the following year. The play was a flop, but Koestler walked into the limelight anyway. Having been criticized by Louis Aragon for his anti-Stalinism, Koestler cancelled a press conference and other public appearances. He spent time meeting old friends, but many others had not survived Nazism.[17]

Koestler also attempted to make friends with the French literary elite. He tracked down Albert Camus in his office at the French publishers Gallimard and they quickly became friends.

He also found Jean-Paul Sartre and Simone de Beauvoir in the Hôtel Pont-Royal. Koestler was the same age as Sartre and only slightly older than Beauvoir, while Camus was eight years younger. Mamaine, who had already met the group on an earlier occasion, joined Koestler in Paris. According to Mamaine, they both got on especially well with Beauvoir.[18] This notable group of thirty- and forty-somethings spent several long nights in each other's company. Koestler was also introduced to other significant figures such as the writer and politician André Malraux, as well as the newly famous Jean Genet. Before leaving Paris, Koestler unwisely slept with Beauvoir. Beauvoir was not particularly eager, Koestler was typically pushy and eight years later Beauvoir was cutting in her fictionalization of the encounter in her novel *The Mandarins* (1954). Mamaine, meanwhile, had become very close to Camus and had an affair with him after Koestler's return to Britain, including a happy week spent in Avignon.[19] Cesarani has written that this visit saw Koestler 'at his worst: opinionated, quarrelsome, snobbish and unfaithful', but this seems unfair. As Koestler wrote to Camus in reference to the affair, he took great liberties in relationships, but also granted them to others.[20]

Koestler and Mamaine spent the next year in Britain. Koestler was hard at work on a non-fictional piece on creativity, humour and emotion, later published as *Insight and Outlook* (1949). Much of his inspiration for the work came from the scientist and philosopher Michael Polanyi. Polanyi, the uncle of Koestler's childhood friend and later girlfriend Eva Striker, had been based in Manchester since 1933. Around Christmas 1945, Polanyi had spent seven weeks in North Wales, close to Koestler's house in the area of Blaenau Ffestiniog, writing three lectures which were later published collectively as *Science, Faith, and Society* (1946). He met with Koestler on numerous occasions during the writing process.[21] Just as Polanyi's niece was decisive for *Darkness at Noon*, Polanyi himself also had a major influence on Koestler's later work. The friendship remained warm and Polanyi was one of Koestler's regular visitors. Many years later, after Michael's death, his wife Magda accused Koestler of having exploited Michael's ideas, but we should not read too much into this, for it appears that the antipathy was mutual.[22] While for his part Michael was more generous, seeing Koestler as 'working in the same vein', Koestler later called Magda her husband's 'worst enemy'.[23]

Dedicated to Mamaine, *Insight and Outlook* claimed to be an 'inquiry into the common foundations of science, art and social ethics', containing 28 chapters on humour, science and the arts, including a lengthy section on what Koestler termed the 'integrative' and 'self-assertive' tendencies. Iain Hamilton termed it a 'very "Middle European" kind of book' due to its thematic breadth and self-conscious erudition.[24] At the end of the book Koestler discusses the particular effect made by contrasts between the tragic and the trivial in a section discussing the story of Jonah as an example of the literary 'night journey' motif.[25] Referring to this passage, James Duban has noted the particular importance of Herman Melville's *Moby-Dick* for Koestler's notion of oceanic wonder.[26]

The ideas discussed in *Insight and Outlook* would be expanded upon in later works (and therefore it will not be discussed in detail here), although at over four hundred pages, the book was already fairly lengthy. Yet the book is evidence of the fact that Koestler's interests were already shifting away from politics. In the early summer of 1947 Koestler became more interested in mysticism, specifically in extrasensory perception and religion, and began reading about yoga. He discovered the work of J. B. Rhine and discussed these topics with Polanyi.[27]

A year after the first trip, Koestler and Mamaine visited Paris again in the autumn of 1947. Relations with Sartre and Beauvoir were at first cordial, but they soon soured as they argued over political differences. Koestler and Mamaine also tried to confront (and were confronted with) French academic snobberies about the

English-speaking world, which Koestler lamented.[28] Beauvoir became especially embittered and thought Koestler was too critical of the Communists and had lent too much support to right-wingers. On another visit to Paris only months later in January 1948, Koestler, Mamaine, Sartre, Beauvoir and Camus all got extremely drunk together, causing a dramatic climax to their friendship. Koestler threw a glass at Sartre, who had made a pass at Mamaine. Meanwhile, Camus and Mamaine were on the verge of tears about the impossibility of their own relationship. Trying to prevent Koestler attacking Sartre, Camus was punched by Koestler. Koestler ran off alone, while the others returned home. A further dimension to these Parisian trips was that Koestler was able to meet Dorothee, to whom he was still married, a fact no doubt of importance to Mamaine, and they now agreed their divorce.[29]

Koestler visited the USA from March to May 1948. It was at this point that his friendship with Eva Striker (by then Eva Zeisel) was interrupted for a number of years. Unable to accept his fierce anti-Communism and the often right-wing figures he now shared a platform with, she turned down the opportunity to speak with him at New York's Carnegie Hall. In reply, Koestler told her that he still felt closer to her than to anyone else in his life. For him, it must have been a particularly difficult break. Of all his friends, he had known Eva the longest; it was through her and her friends that he had first become involved in Communism, and her imprisonment in Moscow had led indirectly to his greatest literary success. But Zeisel refused to give in to the prevailing anti-Communist trend then sweeping America, calling herself a 'non-anticommunist'.[30] It was not the kind of neutral stance that Koestler supported – he was all for taking sides.

According to Mamaine, Koestler struggled with the idea that he was sitting around uselessly when he could be doing something active to improve the lives of others, particularly on the international stage. The issue of the moment was the creation of a Jewish State in Palestine and Koestler and Mamaine had drunk 'solidly all day' to

Koestler with Mamaine Paget. They met in 1944 and lived together in Wales, France, Israel and the USA.

celebrate the United Nations agreement on the partition of Palestine in November 1947.[31] It was the fulfilment of a cause that Koestler had long supported. After a whirlwind U.S. tour during which Koestler was deluged by meetings, interviews and talks, he returned to Britain, and then travelled on to the newly independent state of Israel, which had been declared on 14 May 1948. He wanted to be there on the ground and Mamaine decided to travel with him. They were among the first to obtain visas for the new state, flying over the course of two days by chartered aircraft to Haifa. It was his third extended stay in a country now at war and in the midst of upheaval.

During their stay, Koestler and Mamaine lived in a hotel in Jewish Tel Aviv and met the famous Hungarian photographer Robert Capa

(Endre Friedmann), who advised Mamaine to buy an expensive Leica camera. The timing was once again fateful as the period following Israel's independence was one of the most important phases in the *Nakba*, which is the name given to the flight and expulsion of many hundreds of thousands of Palestinians as a consequence of the war.[32] Koestler even visited some of the newly deserted villages.[33] Mamaine described seeing the corpse of a Syrian officer lying unburied ten days after a skirmish in the mountains.[34] In *The Invisible Writing*, which ostensibly covered his life until 1953, but in practice ends in 1940, Koestler of course does not mention this act of witness. It is another missing chapter in his life story.

Apart from his activities reporting on Israel–Palestine for papers such as the *Manchester Guardian*, *Le Figaro* and the *New York Herald Tribune*, Koestler also tried to influence internal affairs, particularly as regards the status of the Irgun, the Zionist paramilitary group affiliated with Revisionist Zionism. Koestler was horrified at the goings-on in Israel and opposed the actions of the Irgun, the government and Zionist terrorists, as well as of the Mapai, the forerunner of the Israeli Labour Party.[35] Matters came to a head following the sinking of the ship *Altalena* in Tel Aviv. The ship was travelling from France and was carrying 900 men, 5,000 rifles and 270 machine guns as well as anti-tank weapons for use by the Irgun. The Irgun was acting independently of the Israel Defence Forces (IDF), the official army. David Ben-Gurion, then chairman of the provisional government, wanted to suppress the splinter group and ordered the ship to be sunk. Twenty-four were killed in the stand-off between the Irgun and the IDF.[36] Koestler found this act of betrayal very hard to forgive and publicly criticized Ben-Gurion for it, although he went on to interview both him and Menachem Begin, the future Israeli prime minister who was then head of the Irgun.[37]

While Koestler busied himself with Israeli politics, Mamaine was at a loose end in Tel Aviv, eventually leaving for a holiday in Cyprus, and later returning to Britain. The situation in Israel was depressing and there were air raids on Tel Aviv in July. In September, the Swedish UN mediator Folke Bernadotte was murdered in Jerusalem. As 'ghastly' as Tel Aviv was, Mamaine found redeeming aspects of life there too, such as its status as a political hub and its location on the Mediterranean.[38] Fortunately, a solution was at hand as in October 1948 Koestler was invited to France by a Hungarian publisher friend, Paul Winkler. He accepted the invitation and moved to Winkler's chateau near Fontainebleau to write a new book. This was a study of Palestine between 1917 and 1949, titled *Promise and Fulfilment* (1949). Mamaine joined him in France from London and acted as his research assistant.[39] The book is essentially a sustained defence of Israel, providing a non-fictional but no less polemical version of the views Koestler had set out in *Thieves in the Night* and elsewhere.

Having settled back into life in France, Koestler and Mamaine decide to put down roots in Fontainebleau and Koestler bought a house there on the banks of the Seine. It was called Verte Rive and replaced their home in Wales. They frequently invited guests to stay, including the camp survivor Margarete Buber-Neumann. Koestler's next project in the first half of 1949 was a volume of accounts by prominent ex-Communists about their political journeys, titled *The God that Failed: Six Studies in Communism* (1950). The six auto-biographical studies were written by Koestler, Ignazio Silone, André Gide, Richard Wright, Louis Fischer and Stephen Spender. Five were original texts, but because of Gide's declining health, his text was specially adapted from earlier publications. The book appeared in quick succession with *Insight and Outlook* and *Promise and Fulfilment*, but unlike those books was positively reviewed.[40] In his contribution to *The God that Failed*, Koestler stated his view that Nazism and Communism appealed to those Europeans who had been *economically* displaced, people who had considered themselves respectable members of the middle classes but who found themselves without the income to support their lifestyles.

Some refused to accept this situation, 'clung to the empty shell of gentility' and turned to Nazism. Others, like Koestler, felt that they 'lived in a disintegrating society thirsting for faith', and turned to Communism.[41] Koestler described his personal journey from his recruitment to the party to his subsequent disillusionments with it, and talked about the 'intellectual cowardice' of his 'addiction to the Soviet myth', which endured even after he left the party, a spell only broken by the Nazi–Soviet pact.[42]

Life in Fontainebleau was idyllic and Koestler had plenty of ongoing work from all his previous books, some of which were being translated. Mamaine was away for part of the time as she experienced three successive bouts of poor health. Koestler was his usual mix of energy and paranoia, but was still drinking heavily. Ending an already dramatic friendship, Sartre and Beauvoir broke off contact with Koestler and Mamaine because of their ties to the Gaullist André Malraux.[43] One of the most significant developments of the first summer at Verte Rive was Koestler's recruitment of a South African secretary, Cynthia Jefferies, aged 22. Despite the two-decade age gap, Koestler was soon sleeping with her, although he could hardly have guessed that she would later become his third wife. As things stood, he was yet to marry his second: his divorce from Dorothee only came through in December 1949.[44]

Koestler believed strongly in the importance of cultural diplomacy and was recruited by the Congress for Cultural Freedom (ccf) in the autumn of 1949. His friend the author Manès Sperber was involved, as were the academics Sidney Hook and Franz Borkenau, as well as the future *Encounter* editor Melvin Lasky. The ccf was essentially an American-sponsored high-profile cultural summit featuring prominent writers and intellectuals from across Western Europe and America, and supported by figures such as Eleanor Roosevelt and André Gide. It was meant to represent the democratic world's spontaneous response to the burgeoning Cold War. The highlight for Koestler was a speech he gave at the CCF in Berlin in June 1950, which claimed that creating a Western equivalent to the Soviet cultural diplomacy and propaganda effort Cominform was an impossibility. What Koestler did not know then was that the CCF received part of its funding from the CIA. A sharp change in Koestler's attitudes towards the CCF came in August, only a few months later, and seems to have coincided with an attack of delirium tremens from alcohol withdrawal. It is possible that Koestler had discovered the CIA connection, or had realized it, and in his diary he compared the atmosphere to that of 1939.[45] In her book *Who Paid the Piper? The CIA and the Cultural Cold War* (1999), Frances Stonor Saunders claimed that the CIA decided to marginalize Koestler within the CCF, seeing him as a liability.[46] Whichever was the true cause, Koestler withdrew from the CCF's executive committee citing ill health, but continued to support its activities, although without his earlier enthusiasm.

A couple of months before, on 15 April 1950, Koestler had finally married Mamaine at the British Embassy in Paris. Despite the more glamorous location, it was almost as low-key as his previous wedding in Zurich. The day ended in catastrophe when Koestler got very drunk and abandoned Mamaine, leaving her to spend her wedding night at Stephen Spender's flat instead. It was a bad start to a marriage that was destined to be short-lived. Although Koestler tried repeatedly to construct some form of domestic bliss, he kept undermining it through bad behaviour. Mamaine and Koestler were undoubtedly still in love, but things were not looking good.[47] Koestler was also close to finishing a new novel, *The Age of Longing*, which was largely based on his experiences since moving to France. Although not without redeeming aspects, it was a thin novel which became a critical failure.[48]

In August Koestler and Mamaine revisited some of the places Koestler had been to in the South of France during 1940, including Limoges and the foothills of the Pyrenees. In September Koestler

Cold warrior: Koestler speaking at the Congress for Cultural Freedom (CCF), 1950.

stormed out of a private dinner in the Houses of Parliament with the Labour MP Richard Crossman, where they had quarrelled over the future of European integration, social democracy and British isolationism.[49] This was just one of many such stormy ends to evenings with Koestler. Mamaine lists numerous dinner parties that went wrong due to Koestler's outbursts, sulks and stormy exits. Even when he had the upper hand in an argument, such as on this occasion, Koestler struggled to contain his short temper. But it would be wrong to think that Koestler's moodiness made him inherently dislikeable: it may have been part of his attraction. Elizabeth Jane Howard described him later as 'irascible, obsessive, infinitely courageous, a manic depressive, and an idealist'. She also said he had 'an energy whose voltage would have served at least five ordinary people'.[50]

Revisiting America that October, Koestler spontaneously bought a house in Pennsylvania which had been offered at auction. It was a mansion on an island in the Delaware River with seven acres of gardens.[51] Mamaine had grave doubts about moving there with him, but she joined him there at the end of the year. Cracks in their relationship were beginning to show. She was struggling with the burdens Koestler placed on her and had increasingly severe health problems. She also began to consider herself superior to him, not least because she was less neurotic and thin-skinned.[52] Koestler and Mamaine hosted guests most weekends and also visited contacts in Princeton. Koestler had set up a Fund for Intellectual Freedom to support writers from Eastern Europe, which was largely funded with his own money, but helped Eugène Ionesco, among others.[53] It was a time of personal and political confusion because as a left-wing critic of Stalinism, Koestler found himself caught between hardliners on both left and right. He continued to be repeatedly unfaithful to Mamaine, and with the situation worsening, Koestler invited his secretary, Cynthia Jefferies, to join them. This was meant as a solution, but Koestler began sleeping with her again, too.[54] His relations with Cynthia seem to have been similarly stormy, though, as Mamaine describes Koestler as having 'a phobia against poor Cynthia' during one part of her stay in Pennsylvania.[55]

The American interlude lasted just six months. Mamaine returned to England in June 1951, the same month Koestler finally resigned from the CCF. Reunited in Paris in July, Mamaine told Koestler she wanted to leave him, although they at first negotiated a compromise by which they would give America another go. Cynthia was apparently as much a part of the problem, since Mamaine had asked for her to be fired, as, surely, was Koestler's moody behaviour and philandering. Koestler felt both saddened and relieved, and even before Mamaine had left Paris for London he was already seeing someone else. This was Janine Graetz, a Belgian woman married to a German film producer, also known by her maiden name, Detry de Marès.[56] Their relationship would last on and off for several years. Mamaine never did return with Koestler to Pennsylvania and he spent the winter there without her, their relationship finally over. In the first half of 1952, Koestler let the house in America and bought a new one in London, located on Montpelier Square, a five-minute walk from the Harrods department store.

During this period, Koestler had been working on the first volume of his autobiography, *Arrow in the Blue* (1952). As Freadman has written, Koestler's autobiographies can be seen as a 'respondent act', operating in a 'post-totalitarian framework'.[57] Koestler was aware that he had a privileged position from which to comment on mid-twentieth-century politics and society and the interest of his autobiographical work, like that of his fiction, derives largely from this. Despite the attention given to his novels, Koestler's autobiographies belong to his best works. *Dialogue with Death*, for example, has been described as 'autobiography of the most intimate and compelling kind'.[58] *Arrow in the Blue* describes his childhood in Budapest and Vienna and his involvement with the Zionist movement, as well as how he became a journalist. It follows his story up until the point at which he decided to join the Communist Party in 1931.

In Koestler's view all autobiographers have a common motive, namely to 'transcend the isolation of the self'. He identifies two different reasons for doing so, which he terms the 'Chronicler's urge' and the 'Ecce Homo motive' (the Latin *ecce homo*, from John 19:5, is conventionally translated as 'Behold the man!') (*AB*, p. 29). The chronicler aims to share his experience of events in the outside world, while the man-to-be-beholden wants to share his internal life. Koestler believed he was a chronicler, but was motivated to some degree by both wishes; he wanted to chronicle his experiences of imprisonment during the Spanish Civil War, and also to have an enduring reputation as a writer, to still be read a century later (*AB*, pp. 31–2). This, he says, is where the two urges meet. Primarily, then, Koestler set out to be a chronicler, but he was also interested in sharing his internal life. When Scammell writes that *Arrow in the Blue* is 'not a memoir of self-revelation in the sense that the form came to be understood in the late twentieth century', he is only repeating what Koestler had already indicated. However, Scammell also sees Koestler as an 'exemplary' exponent of the 'ecce homo' genre, praising his 'self-analysis and the honesty of some of his self-descriptions' in particular.[59] Stephen Spender, however, was less impressed. Writing in 1952, he criticized the book for being 'theory-ridden'.[60]

Arrow in the Blue was published in 1952 and was followed two years later by a second volume, titled *The Invisible Writing*, which covers the years 1931–53. This is an account of Koestler's prompt ejection from the newspaper industry after having become a Communist, his travels in the Soviet Union and his later experiences in Budapest and Paris. He provides less detail on his experiences in Spain in 1936–7, which he recounts in *Spanish Testament* and the book stops short of his experiences in France in 1940–41, as told in *Scum of the Earth*. Although the book is titled as an autobiography to 1953, Koestler hardly talks about the last twelve years. An epilogue fills in some of the next decade, but provides little detail. The combined length of the two volumes is over seven hundred pages, making Koestler's autobiography notable for its length, as well as its consistent quality.

However, Koestler was not able to enjoy his achievement. Before Koestler's *The Invisible Writing* was published, events in the present day took an unexpected and unhappy turn. Following their divorce the previous year, his ex-wife Mamaine died in London's University College Hospital on 1 June 1954. Neither Koestler nor Mamaine's twin sister had been aware of how ill she had become. Mamaine had been suffering from bad asthma and the cause of death was given as 'exhaustion', although in reality this meant multiple organ failure.[61] Her death plunged Koestler into crisis, as he blamed himself for treating her badly and neglecting her.

Mamaine's was a tragic but remarkable story. When Koestler met her in January 1944, he had been impressed by her beauty, independence and intelligence. A fluent speaker of French and German, Mamaine was well read and well connected. Her hobbies included playing the piano and she was a keen amateur bird-watcher. She loved to read, and wrote with particular enthusiasm about the work of Simone Weil, which she read in the French original.[62] Almost throughout their relationship, Mamaine had endured bouts of chronic asthma, bronchitis and flu. In the bad times, her relationship with Koestler was marred by his poor behaviour. He hit her more than once, there were frequent arguments and he was often critical of her shortcomings.[63] Their intercontinental lifestyle also took its toll and Mamaine described the 'intense boredom of travelling around with someone famous'.[64] At other times she was an admirer and supporter of Koestler and could have left him for several other men had she wished to. She chose, albeit sometimes reluctantly, to accompany him to Palestine, France and America and was often happy with him, telling Celia that she would consider her life 'well spent' because of the years she had spent with him.[65] Mamaine was at ease in Koestler's social circle. She met Sartre, Beauvoir and Camus before he did, and even after they separated maintained an independent correspondence with his friends, including Manès Sperber. However, in the months leading up to her death she was admitted to hospital several times, and wrote to Sperber telling of her ill health, loneliness and depression.[66]

Matters were made worse for Koestler by the fact that in the year leading up to her death he had only seen her occasionally and had had two new relationships, one with Janetta Jackson and the other with Janine Detry de Marès. He had travelled to Austria with

Jackson and offered to marry her, and at the time of Mamaine's death, Koestler was living on the Italian island of Ischia with Detry de Marès. Koestler had first visited Ischia the previous autumn and had bought a holiday home there with her. Although he moved in with Detry de Marès after Mamaine's death, his grief meant that they lived in the Ischia home for only a month. He left the island and asked Detry de Marès to sell the house. Around the same time, his Pennsylvanian home Island Farm was also sold. Koestler was clearly trying to turn over a new leaf, as soon afterwards he also handed over responsibility for his Fund for Intellectual Freedom, now four years old, to International PEN.[67] Koestler also began to consider giving up political writing and activism, making a note to this effect in his diary later that year.[68]

In London in the autumn of 1954, Detry de Marès told Koestler that she was pregnant and that he was the father. Koestler had no particular reason to doubt it. She wanted to keep the baby and her new husband (the 7th Earl of Warwick) would recognize the child as his. They argued but Koestler remained adamant that he did not want a child; nor did he want to continue his relationship with Janine. He started a relationship with the novelist Elizabeth Jane Howard in February 1955, which was still going on when Detry de Marès's daughter, named Cristina, was born in April. According to Scammell, today Cristina no longer believes that Koestler was her father at all.[69] While it is difficult to empathize with Koestler's cold rejection of the child he was told was his, it is also no surprise that when Howard told him she was pregnant just two months later, Koestler was horrified and asked Howard to have an abortion. She did not want to at first, but agreed to it later. The abortion brought the relationship to an end in the unhappiest way possible: Howard was left alone to recover while Koestler took off for the weekend. The story was told by Howard, as part of a particularly perceptive portrait of Koestler's selfishness and his brilliance, in her *Slipstream: A Memoir* (2002). Howard also included words of praise, writing, 'Sometimes I dreaded being alone with him. Sometimes I loved him very much. Always I felt spellbound.'[70]

Just over a year after Mamaine's death, Koestler became involved with the campaign to end the death penalty in Britain. He re-employed Cynthia to work as an assistant on the project and spent the summer of 1955 working busily on the project, finishing the manuscript of what would become *Reflections on Hanging* in October. He invited Cynthia back to work for him the following month, and contributed articles against hanging under the pseudonym 'Vigil' to the British weekly *The Observer*. After the end of his relationship with Howard, Koestler started to pursue the author Joan Henry, who had written a memoir about prison life called *Who Lie in Gaol* (1952) and a novel about death row titled *Yield to the Night* (1954). Koestler asked Henry to marry him, but she laughed it off and told him he should marry Cynthia instead.[71] Koestler did not see Cynthia as wife material and she was essentially being used. Cynthia had had an abortion without anaesthetic at a secret clinic in March 1956 but he showed no sign of committing to her, despite her obvious devotion.[72] Given Koestler's private approach to the matter, his statement on the high abortion rate in Japan in *The Lotus and the Robot* (1960), which he describes as 'the slaughter of the unborn', is surprising to say the least (*LR*, p. 168). But at least the next time Cynthia had an abortion, in November 1962, it was at a proper clinic.

The winter also saw the publication of an essay collection titled *The Trail of the Dinosaur*, which made waves for a previously unpublished piece outlining Koestler's views on Jewish identity. Titled 'Judah at the Crossroads', the text expounded Koestler's belief that there needed to be an end to Jewish otherness. Aside from claiming that Judaism is 'racially discriminatory, nationally segregative, socially tension-creating' (*TD*, p. 111), Koestler also described his own reasons for engaging with Zionist politics deriving from his family background, namely his desire to create a 'haven for the persecuted and homeless' Jews, something he considered fulfilled in 1948 (*TD*, p. 122). In many ways it served as a public renunciation of the identity with which he had been labelled since birth, one which he, like other secular Jews, clearly felt 'unable to define . . . in either racial or religious terms' (*TD*, p. 114), an intellectually dissatisfying reality that he was reluctant to accept. The postmodern use of hybridity or diaspora as metaphors for understanding identity would evidently not have been to Koestler's liking.

A pamphlet by Koestler, writing as 'Vigil', titled 'Patterns of Murder' was circulated to Members of Parliament, in which he listed individually the 85 people hanged in Britain between 1949 and 1953, many of whom may have been mentally ill, some of whom were unjustly convicted, and more than a third were under the age of 25. In the pamphlet's conclusions, Koestler repeatedly sought to bolster his case that hanging the mentally ill was 'morally indefensible'.[73] *Reflections on Hanging* was published in April 1956 and was well received.[74] Hanging had played a part in Koestler's pre-war journalistic career too. As he detailed in *Arrow in the Blue*, in the Weimar era, the Ullstein papers had been opposed to capital punishment, but the editorial committee forced their journalists not to protest the death sentence passed in 1931 on the murderer and rapist Fritz Haarmann. The incident frightened Koestler, because he saw in it the capitulation of a principled newspaper to an increasingly radicalized readership (*AB*, pp. 223–4). Returning to the issue with twenty years of hindsight, the essential point of Koestler's book is that hanging is a brutal practice that is also an ineffective deterrent to criminals. Referring to the history of capital punishment in Britain and its then comparatively barbaric justice compared to its European neighbours, as well as specific cases and parliamentary debates, Koestler argued that hanging (and, indeed, capital punishment) was a savage and inhuman practice.

Koestler's discussion was centred on the tension between free will and determinism (a favourite topic of Koestler's, on which his opinion was never wholly clear).[75] In a section titled 'Free Will and Determinism: The Philosophy of Hanging', Koestler suggested that the intractability of the philosophical debate on the existence of free will was reason enough to abolish capital punishment. Beginning with the question as to whether we really have choices about our actions, a question which he said had largely been avoided in debates on capital punishment, Koestler went on to argue that criminal responsibility was essentially a theological idea dependent on some kind of metaphysical entity. The logic behind his argument is that science supports deterministic theories of cause and effect and that the notion of freedom is at worst illusory, at best only a negative 'freedom from', rather than a 'freedom to'. Whether one accepts this view or not, Koestler felt that capital punishment was too blunt an instrument to deal with the intricacies of each specific crime, let alone with the debate on the existence of God and/or free will (R, pp. 92–102).

In some ways it was the culmination of his engagement with the topic of incarceration and the penal system dating back to his imprisonment in the Spanish Civil War some twenty years before. Koestler's own footnote to his argument, where he speaks of a 'factor' that determines 'an order of reality' in which 'the present is *not* determined by the past' (R, p. 102), is indicative of the centrality of the debate among Koestler's ideas. In her diary, Mamaine recalled Koestler describing this as 'the intervention of a hidden variable'.[76] It is another instance of Koestler's recourse to mysticism, in itself a political and philosophical gesture, which is one of the notable features of *Spanish Testament / Dialogue with Death* and many later works. As Richard Freadman and Matthew Taunton have convincingly argued, Koestler's conflation of the rationalist disciplines of science and mathematics with mysticism is his way of resisting the cause-and-effect logic of authoritarianism.[77]

In the summer of 1956, the bill to abolish capital punishment was rejected by the House of Lords. The campaign had failed, but reform would prove unstoppable and Koestler had helped drive the point home.

5

Science and Progress

Koestler had a passion to see the irrational world in scientific terms and to seek out the irrational elements in science. Ultimately this led him to apply a limited vocabulary to an infinite problem. In the two decades following the campaign against hanging, Koestler's ideas on free will progressed from the 'Philosophy of Hanging' towards a holistic theory of everything. As Stephen Toulmin put it in 1968, 'Intellectual courage and imagination on this scale are, in themselves, rare and admirable; but has there not been something misguided about the whole thing?'[1] Toulmin neatly summarizes the dilemma that has plagued many of the readers of Koestler's later work. Koestler became concerned with debates on the transferability or interdisciplinary application of scientific knowledge, particularly ideas in the philosophy of science on what is known as 'reductionism'. He even tried to see these debates in the context of the Cold War and the nuclear threat in particular, building up a picture of a flawed human race that had doomed itself to extinction (*J*, pp. 1–5). And it is from these shifts of topic and the sheer ambition of his project that the sense of the misguidedness of Koestler's work derives.

Beginning with the earlier work *Insight and Outlook*, Koestler developed two concepts which recur as the pillars of his universal theory in his later work. The first was the idea of the 'holon', a term to describe the individual units of natural systems, and the second was the notion of 'bisociation', meaning something similar to cognitive dissonance. In using them, Koestler was anxious to draw analogies between biology, sociology and psychology, all the while never losing sight of the philosophical debate on free will and metaphysics. He passionately believed that science needed to remain open to the possibility of metaphysical phenomena, particularly to the possibility of telepathy, as well as to the high likelihood of extraterrestrial life. As he stated, 'a true science of life must let infinity in and never lose sight of it' (*GM*, p. 220).

Koestler would later liken his shift in interests to a sex change and described his new adventure as an 'intellectual armchair odyssey'.[2] In 1956, though, the 51-year-old Koestler was still perceived as mainly a political writer, one who exemplified the 'value of pressing dreams into the service of criticism'.[3] Yet one of the most strident opinions Koestler had expressed in his autobiography was his condemnation of the tendency of middle-class 'intellectuals' to cultivate snobberies about the arts, affecting understanding and knowledge of them, while taking a perverse pride in not understanding the natural sciences and mathematics. Koestler thought that this led to a form of estrangement caused by intellectual laziness or passivity (*AB*, p. 50). Of course, he did not put himself in this category. With Cynthia as a faithful assistant, Koestler intended to return to science writing, the career he had left behind when he travelled to the Soviet Union. Whether this was a good decision or not has been fought over ever since, with even his 'official' biographer, Michael Scammell, speculating as to whether it might not have been better if Koestler had 'died in his forties . . . instead of sullying his career with speculations about astronomy, evolution, parapsychology, and Jewish racial theories'.[4]

Before embarking on the campaign against hanging, Koestler had already started work on a biography of Johannes Kepler, even visiting Kepler's birthplace in Germany, but had put it on hold. He now devoted himself fully to the project. Having spent a summer in Wiltshire, he marked a new phase in his life by buying a house

Koestler on his armchair odyssey, 1960. Portrait by Karoly Forgacs.

in the Kent countryside, a timber-framed house with two wings called Long Barn.[5] Remarkably, the house was where Vita Sackville-West and Harold Nicholson created their first major garden before Sissinghurst. It was therefore the model of English country style and the perfect place for an aspiring public intellectual to settle down.

Predictably, though, the idyll did not last long. Political events almost immediately created a significant diversion from his new studies and environs. The Hungarian Revolution which began in October 1956 was brutally suppressed in the first week of November by Soviet troops. Koestler remained active behind the scenes and briefly played host to a family of Hungarian refugees. He campaigned privately to increase public awareness of the imprisonment of the writers Julius Hay and Tibor Déry and personally asked Hugh Gaitskell, then leader of the Labour Party, to put a word in on Déry's behalf on a visit to Moscow.[6] Staying true to his 'new' career, however, he made no public statement.

The year of 1957 was spent working on *The Sleepwalkers*, which had expanded from a book simply about Kepler. Like its predecessor, the book drew on some of the ideas of Michael Polanyi, who like

Koestler built a house in Alpbach in the late 1950s, the Austrian village home to the European Forum. Pictured here with Erwin Schrödinger, 1957.

Koestler was interested in links between science and faith.[7] In keeping with his new theme, Koestler took part in the European Forum Alpbach, an annual and high-profile festival of ideas, in the summer of 1957. It was there that he met Eva Auer, a Viennese painter and the wife of the conference organizer. They soon began an affair.[8] Whether as a result of his new relationship or not, by the end of 1957 his relationship with Cynthia was on the rocks. Koestler finished *The Sleepwalkers* in March 1958, and spent much of the rest of the year arranging for a Tyrolean chalet to be built for him in Alpbach, the Austrian mountain village that has hosted the European Forum since 1945. Although he kept his London home, the move was also a kind of reorientation towards the Continent and Koestler sold his archetypal English country home, Long Barn, in 1959.

What did Koestler's decision to settle in Alpbach, at least temporarily, say about his relationship to Austria, a country in which he was at least partially a native? When Koestler had first revisited Vienna he was disappointed and depressed by how provincial the city had become, telling a friend that even Haifa seemed metropolitan in comparison.[9] Koestler had expected something more like the Vienna of the 1920s, which he had known before the political repressions, the ethnic cleansing and the war.

Koestler could hardly escape his Austrian side, even if some commentators have not perceived him as Austrian. Cesarani imagined Koestler as out of place in Alpbach, a 'short, stout Hungarian Jew trying to be a thigh-slapping Tyrolean peasant'.[10] This seems an impossible line to take, as there was no sense that Austrian culture was particularly foreign to Koestler. Koestler did feel a connection to Hungary and never lost touch with its culture; Pál Ignotus speculated that the fact his works were not available in Hungarian upset Koestler during his lifetime.[11] At the same time, Koestler was half-Austrian by birth, and spent formative years in Baden and Vienna, as well as in Budapest. Furthermore, the alpine resort of Alpbach was hardly the 'authentic' countryside. Joseph Strelka, who met Koestler, said that he had no trace of a Hungarian accent in any of his foreign languages. He spoke English like a German and German with an English twang, using the pronunciation of the Berlin dialect in conjunction with the idioms of Vienna.[12] He makes the additional point that Koestler's mother tongue, in the most literal sense, was also German, as he had an Austrian mother.[13] Alpbach was also a place where Koestler could socialize with other prominent Austrian exiles, such as Erwin Schrödinger.[14] When Karl Popper was in Alpbach, Koestler offered to show him round the house he built there, the so-called Schreiberhäusl or writer's house.[15] He counted Michael Polanyi and Friedrich von Hayek as regular visitors and, writing to Ludwig von Bertalanffy, said, 'As you can see, we are great Höhenluft ['mountain air'] snobs.'[16]

If returning to Austria after the war brought with it a certain nostalgia for the ethnic diversity of pre-war Vienna, Koestler was also positive about the country's future. He was matter-of-fact about the post-war embrace of political stasis via conservative-social democratic coalitions and saw the parties' extension of all-pervasive zones of influence as the lesser evil, given the country's history since 1918. He saw the Russian occupation of eastern Austria, which ended only a year before the Hungarian Revolution of 1956, as a particularly traumatic moment in the national psyche that had cured the country of Communist sympathies for good. Yet in light of the Austrians' willingness to help the Hungarian refugees in 1956 and in their enduring Commitment to high culture, Koestler predicted that the 'spirit of Vienna' would prevail (*DI*, pp. 135–40).

The publication of *The Sleepwalkers: A History of Man's Changing Vision of the Universe* came in 1959. The book was briefly successful, perhaps helped by the fact that Koestler was already famous.[17] From its starting point as a biography, it became a much more broadly conceived book about the history of scientific discovery, oriented around the once revolutionary notion that the earth orbits around the sun, known as heliocentrism. It began with the story of Pythagoras as well as ancient Greek and Roman theories of heliocentrism; it then moved on to the theological ideas of the Middle Ages and the discoveries of Copernicus, and from there to the stories of Kepler and Galileo. Koestler hoped to tell the story of the competition between scientific and religious understandings of the world and to investigate the process of discovery through life stories. He tried to portray science as a Janus-faced entity caught dialectically between empirical and mystical tendencies (*SW*, pp. 14–15).

Koestler thought that the history of science had paid too little attention to its own psychological or affective history, the questions of personality and personal history that have been crucial in its development. His intention was not to 'debunk' his subjects, but to see their creative lives in a rounded biographical context. He described how as a child he had thought the plaster figures on the ceiling of their Budapest apartment were gods, and in the book went on to describe various metaphors for the universe, from Babylon onwards. He stated the belief that astronomy and astrology could be seen as having shared interests (*sw*, p. 21). This boils down to the psychologically rational idea that patterns in mathematics, as well as in astronomy, seem to point towards divine order and harmony, as in the Pythagorean system.

Koestler argued that far from being victims of their own ignorance, many scientists of the past were frequently too afraid or too cowardly to draw the right conclusions from the evidence they had before them. For him the history of science was by no means a story of continuous progress, but one in which long periods of inactivity and stasis are punctuated by extraordinary advances (*sw*, pp. 70–79). One reason Koestler saw for the stasis in scientific development was the separation of religion from science, which he described as 'the denial of science as a way of worship' (*sw*, p. 85). He understood that the way a society thinks about the universe is deeply political, the latter essentially a reflection of the former (*sw*, p. 103). For Koestler, the split between science and religion was made unavoidable following the decree against heliocentric theories made during the first trial of Galileo in 1616 (*sw*, p. 456).

Koestler is far from hagiographic in his portrayal of the scientists who made history. Koestler's title *The Sleepwalkers* referred to the way in which much scientific progress was made unwittingly, or through happy coincidence. According to Koestler, Copernicus had the 'intuition of the original genius', which is to say he had the right idea, but failed to elaborate on it correctly (*sw*, p. 202). Kepler, too, seemed not to realize the impact his work would have and thought he had proven things which he had not (*sw*, p. 325; p. 396). Copernicus was 'an old sourpuss', Kepler was a 'neurotic child from a problem-family', while Galileo was accused of 'sophistry, evasion and plain dishonesty' (*sw*, p. 185; p. 237; p. 439). Koestler did not see the scientists' shortcomings as a problem, however; nor did he lament their mistakes. For him, the value of these scientists' contributions was not really in what they discovered, but in the disruptive questions that they asked and the responses they generated (*sw*, p. 263).

The Sleepwalkers was published the same year as C. P. Snow's famous lecture 'The Two Cultures', delivered in Cambridge in May 1959, which serves as an illustration of how Koestler's work connected with the contemporary zeitgeist. Just as Koestler had in his autobiography, Snow highlighted the fact that middle-class 'literary intellectuals', particularly those in Britain, were ignorant of even the basics of natural science. And, in a way similar to Raymond Williams, whose book *Culture and Society* was published the previous year, Snow conceived of this in terms of social inequality. He predicted a time when the West would become poorer owing to its failure to keep pace in the domains of science and technology. Throughout 'The Two Cultures', which Snow later said he wished he had titled 'The Rich and the Poor', there is a strong sense of the Western world facing new challenges in a globalizing world. For Snow, the scientific revolution offered people the hope of three basic 'primal' things: 'years of life, freedom from hunger, survival for children'.[18]

While Thomas Kuhn's seminal *The Structure of Scientific Revolutions* (1962) also discussed Kepler, it studiously avoids mentioning Koestler's *The Sleepwalkers*. Koestler's contribution was no doubt too 'popular' to warrant mentioning, but the shared interest of the books in describing what it means to make progress in science is clear. Kuhn, who is responsible for establishing the notion of 'paradigm shifts' in the history of science, achieved what Koestler did not, namely a real landmark in the academic history of science (recently celebrated with a 'fiftieth anniversary' edition).[19] Yet many of the phenomena Kuhn outlined are pre-empted in different ways in Koestler's book, which is more historically curious, more biographical, more interested in the two cultures debate than Kuhn's, and is, like *The Structure of Scientific Revolutions*, still in print.[20]

Like C. P. Snow, Koestler was also thinking about globalization, particularly in its cultural form. His next book project was *The Lotus and the Robot*, a fusion of travel writing and intellectual history, which he completed in May 1960 and which was published the same year. On the invitation of the CCF, Koestler had made a trip to India and Japan around New Year 1959, and took the opportunity to contrast Western intellectual culture with that of the democratic East.[21] *The Lotus and the Robot* is partly an anecdotal account of Koestler's stays in India and Japan, but it is also a Euro-centric critique of the place of traditional Asian cultural and religious theories in a globalizing world. Koestler was sympathetic to mysticism to an extent, but only if scientific explanation had been exhausted (*LR*, p. 12). He considered the notion of Asian spiritualism as a source of insight to be anachronistic, and thought the American-ization of Asia, like the Americanization of Europe, was at heart consumer-led and spontaneous. Although he lamented that mass culture led to dumbing down, he argued that what he termed 'coca-colonization' (that is, increasing cultural uniformity) was inevitable and unstoppable. He considered the ubiquitous contrast between Eastern spirituality and Western materialism to be fallacious, and hinted that both the Western rationalist tradition and Asian mysticism were equally arrogant in their rejection of the other. However, his European sympathies were made clear when he described the Renaissance and Enlightenment as the true origins of intellectual and cultural progress in the contemporary world. Similarly, the Arab or Jewish stewardship of the Greek tradition during the Dark Ages was insignificant, as it was only Europe that was able to revivify the dormant pursuit of knowledge. Koestler came back from Asia an unapologetic European (*LR*, pp. 278–85).

In his account of India, Koestler was mildly critical of figures such as Ghandi's 'spiritual successor' Vinoba Bhave, the leader of the Bhoodan movement for voluntary land reform, as well as the guru Sri Atmananda Krishna Menon, who died not long after Koestler's stay. However, his harshest criticism was reserved for traditional yogic teachings on physiology, particularly as concerns bodily fluids. At times, the tone of Koestler's account comes close to mockery, particularly when he details at length some of the incredible ideas propagated as part of yogic doctrine about digestive health and the ability not only to mentally control ejaculation and excretion, but to retract semen into the penis (*LR*, pp. 87–96). While he made light of yogic doctrine, his intention was serious. He perceived a crisis in Indian sexual politics that derived from a deep ambivalence about the body and sex within Hinduism, which celebrated sex while also making it taboo. Even Ghandi, otherwise a practitioner of tolerance, seemed to Koestler to exhibit these characteristic sexual hang-ups (*LR*, p. 138; p. 150).

Koestler was shocked by the social impact of urbanization in India. He hypothesized that the emphasis on obedience in Indian traditional culture, combined with its taboo about sex, led to a perfect storm as far as social alienation in cities was concerned (*LR*, pp. 155–7). But Koestler was also interested in the way that in the Hindu and Buddhist traditions, rationality and spirituality had not been separated, as had occurred in Christianity (*LR*, p. 50). If Koestler had hoped that he would find support in India for his ideas of 'science-as-worship', explored not only in *The Sleepwalkers* but in his 'arrow in the blue' metaphor in his autobiographies, he was to be disappointed. At least for Koestler's interviewees, science was still a way of proving religion right, as it had been for the medieval Catholic Church, and this attitude was fundamentally incompatible with Koestler's view that mysticism begins only where science fails (*LR*, p. 59). The Eastern tradition was in his view anti-empirical and lacked a theory of physical causation, being based on the notion that the perceiving subject and the perceived object were 'a single, indivisible, fluid reality' (*LR*, p. 43; p. 113). The two traditions were in his view fundamentally incompatible, with attempts at synthesis producing 'a game of Wonderland croquet with mobile hoops' (*LR*, pp. 49–50).

Japan was more to Koestler's liking than India, but he found certain aspects of Japanese life frustrating and troubling. He moaned about the ubiquity of piped music, whether from pleasure boats or portable radios, and was critical of the Japanese trust in mood-altering medication. While he admired Japanese culture, he also found it static and ossified, but it was its Westernized aspects that he found most disturbing. He compared the ideal image of Japan ('lotusland') with the intensification and exaggeration of Western habits ('robotland'), and suggested this was the reason for many Westerners' love-hate responses to the country. While its past and culture seemed attractive, this illusion was frequently punctured by the confrontation with an unflattering mirror image of the West itself (*LR*, p. 173).

As in the case of Indian spirituality, Koestler was sceptical about the teachings of Zen Buddhism. He echoed the frequent criticism that it was an essentially amoral religion, which did not differentiate between right and wrong (*LR*, p. 272). He did not think that there was much in the way of true religious feeling in Japan and was sceptical about the ability of Zen Buddhism to provide a moral compass in the post-war setting. On the other hand, he professed his fascination for the particular tension between perfectionism and evasiveness that he thought characterized Japanese culture, and wrote that if he were ever to have to leave Europe for whatever reason in the future, Japan would be the country where he would most prefer to be a foreigner (*LR*, pp. 274–5).

In the summer of 1960 Koestler was once again in Alpbach, but he received news that his mother was dying and so flew back from Austria to visit her one last time before her death.[22] His relationship with her had always been strained, but her own background was not easy. Before Koestler's birth, Adele's father had emigrated from Vienna to New York under mysterious circumstances, perhaps owing to a financial scandal, while Adele and her mother had been forced to move to live with her sister in Budapest.[23] Although she never left Henrik, her marriage was often fraught and both Henrik and Adele may have had other lovers.[24] In her relationship with her son, she was at times a controlling person and often expressed her need for more attention. On the other hand, Arthur did try to avoid his mother and she undoubtedly noticed this. Having assumed her to be killed in Auschwitz and racked by worry during the war, even to the point that he initially put his relationship with Mamaine on hold, Koestler did little to build a constructive relationship with Adele thereafter.

At one point he wrote in his diary that he pitied his mother, but having been convinced by his psychoanalyst that Adele was the ultimate cause of his insecurities, he showed little sympathy for her situation. Perhaps he had reason, as the evidence suggests she was a difficult woman. According to Mamaine, Adele told Arthur that she had received 'hundreds' of food parcels in Hungary, meaning that her previous story of terrible hardship was exaggerated.[25] The usually charming Mamaine disliked Adele and wrote that she never listened to and could not understand their conversations.[26] Adele was invited to stay with Arthur and Mamaine at Fontainebleau in the summers of 1949 and 1951, but she was hurt by his representation of his child-hood in *The God that Failed*. Koestler was unrepentant, and the portrayal in *Arrow in the Blue* was certainly no more complimentary.[27] Adele also disapproved of Koestler and Mamaine's breakup.[28] Koestler hardly saw Adele in the final year of her life, although he was with her when she died. There were not many people at her funeral, possibly because Koestler did not inform anyone.[29]

In January 1961 Koestler travelled to San Francisco to take part in a symposium on 'Control of the Mind'. It was on this trip that

Koestler tried psilocybin, the active ingredient in magic mushrooms, on two separate occasions. He also used the trip to visit J. B. Rhine at Duke University to learn more about his work on parapsychology. Later that year, he undertook experiments at home to try and discover whether weight loss was possible through hypnosis.[30] Koestler wrote about his experiences with drugs in an essay titled 'Return Trip to Nirvana', first published in the *Sunday Telegraph* in March. The first of the experiments took place at the University of Michigan at Ann Arbor. Koestler took nine small pills and the effects kicked in after about an hour. With closed eyes he saw patterns and strange images of worms that transformed into dragons. With his eyes open, his senses became distorted. Background noise became dominant, barely noticeable lights seemed to take on special meaning and people's faces became grotesquely distorted. On his second experiment in Boston, there were again spatial distortions, but the faces of those around him became more beautiful and listening to music seemed incredibly profound. Koestler did not rate his experiences. He found the visions too cheaply obtained and the apparent insights seemed superficial when sobriety kicked back in (*DI*, pp. 201–12).

In 1961 Cynthia was still on the scene, although her relationship with Koestler had been anything but easy. In the course of the previous years she had been distanced, thrown out of the London flat, asked to move back in and then left to live in the attic in Alpbach. After this rough patch, Cynthia was later more closely integrated into his life again and began to try to live up to Koestler's highly patriarchal view of a woman's place. He even asked her to take cookery lessons in order to better entertain his guests. It was intended as a permanent shift. Although they were not yet married, like Mamaine before her, Cynthia now changed her name to Koestler.[31]

As he moved on from the history of science towards its philosophy, Koestler came to rely on two words, 'holon' and 'bisociation', which he hoped would enter the English language (neither have). The 'holon' should really be understood as Koestler's response to the question of reductionism. Reductionism is a topic in the philosophy of science, particularly the philosophy of biology, and it concerns the possibility of transferring scientific models from one discipline to another. Can biological organisms be understood using structures from physics and chemistry? Is 'life' something more than molecules and chemical reactions? What does biology tell us about other branches of science?

Koestler's 'holons' went further than any professional scientist would probably feel comfortable with in theoretical terms. He imagined a radical interdisciplinarity where not only the natural sciences but the human and life sciences shared common structural features. His ideas had echoes of a utopian dream of a universal theory of knowledge, but Koestler said he was opposed to the oversimplification of complex science. It reduced sophisticated processes to 'nothing but' more basic ones found in less advanced organisms, as when experiments on rats are used to draw conclusions about humans (*J*, pp. 25–6). He also believed that the prevalence of such ideas could be ascribed to the scientist's desire to believe that, in time, all the mysteries of the universe can be explained, which he referred to as the 'rationalist fallacy' (*J*, p. 278). But if the sum of Koestler's work is taken into account, it becomes clear that he applied the same model to humour as to biological organization, artistic creativity, scientific discovery and para-psychology. He fell victim to the same fallacy, albeit in defence of the universe's mystery.

There are, of course, different forms of reductionism – put simply, not only whether models can be shifted laterally between disciplines, but whether conclusions can be generalized 'upwards' or 'downwards' between different levels of biological hierarchies.[32] Koestler wanted to argue against bottom-up 'nothing-but-ism', which reduces higher-level processes to the sum of its lower-level parts. His understanding was akin to that of Goethe, whose notion of the originary plant or *Urpflanze* was supposed to facilitate reflection on plants as entire organisms, rather than just amalgamations of lower-level features.[33]

Koestler's own theory relies on the notion that 'wholes' break down into 'parts' in hierarchic ways that are essentially analogous to one another. Crucially, each level in the hierarchy was to be understood as also constituting a whole, and these sub-wholes are what Koestler dubbed 'holons' (*J*, p. 27). Holons are therefore wholes which are always also parts. Koestler imagined them as being governed by two principles, 'the self-assertive tendency' and the 'integrative tendency'. In asserting itself, the holon is perceived as a whole. Seen within the context of the system, the holon is just a part integrated into another entity. For this reason, Koestler saw these sub-wholes as 'Janus-faced' (*J*, p. 27; p. 78).

Koestler was interested by what made the upper levels of the biological hierarchy – for example, the sheer complexity and power of the human brain – more than just the product of a Darwinian evolutionary process. At the same time, he believed that the human brain's apparent overdevelopment could not be explained in traditional Darwinian terms. 'Bisociation' was at the core of Koestler's answer. It was the term Koestler came up with to explain humour in terms of the interaction of psychology, culture and biology, laughter being a uniquely human physical reflex that can be triggered by mental activity (by processing funny aural or visual information). His theory was that humour derives from the parallel perception of a particular piece of information, a mental holon, in two mutually incompatible contexts (*J*, pp. 113–14). For example, he identified bisociative logic at work in anthropomorphism and zoomorphism, comparing the duality of animals in fiction behaving like humans to the way caricatures emphasize grotesque or animal-like features in human faces. More importantly, bisociation underpinned creative processes, being a way of describing what occurs when the brain utilizes associative logic to make links between different contexts. As such, bisociation could be said to be the process that underpins all scientific discovery (*J*, p. 123; p. 132).

If this seems like a lot of information to pack into a short paragraph, then it should give a flavour of the breadth of Koestler's ambition and the lengths he went to in order to make his ideas seem credible (the irony being that, had he restricted himself to essays or shorter, less demonstratively 'scholarly' books, he may have been perceived as a Continental philosopher, rather than as an academic wannabe). It is difficult not to interpret Koestler's desire to write very long, pseudo-academic books in terms of an insecurity about his own educational background. Koestler had, after all, abandoned his engineering degree in Vienna and had never graduated. Making an entrance into a subject area where you have no particular expertise, except a professional journalistic interest in science, and hoping to contribute to it philosophically is at the very least a self-assertive (and not an integrative) act. In his own autobiographical account, Koestler was fascinated by the idea of the infinite, to the extent, with his 'arrow in the blue' metaphor, that it even made humanitarian disasters fade into insignificance. His later obsession with writing about science could be seen as responding to an autobiographical story about himself, as a self-staging by an anxious man.

Koestler was still in the process of writing his longest book on the subject, *The Act of Creation*, but he also got involved with two very different causes. The year 1962 saw the first award of a ground-breaking new prize for prison arts called the Koestler Award, based on an idea Koestler had had in 1960.[34] The Koestler Trust still exists today, and describes itself as the 'UK's best-known prison arts charity'.

The other was the campaign to abolish quarantine for dogs, a proposed reform which eventually became reality in 2001 with the introduction of 'pet passports'.[35] This interest of Koestler clearly raised eyebrows in some circles and at Christmas that year, he argued bitterly with his friend the novelist Henry Green, whom he accused of being anti-Semitic over comments he made. Another witness said that Koestler had misunderstood, and that the comments had been directed at Koestler's articles on quarantine.[36]

In 1963 Koestler wrote some anti-establishment essays about Britain and in one of them called for the abolition of private schools. This intervention led to a special issue of *Encounter* responding to George Orwell's *The Lion and the Unicorn*, but titled *The Lion and the Ostrich.* These are perennial questions within British society. Hamilton reaffirmed their relevance to public debates on inequality in 1980 and thirty years later little seems to have changed.[37] In Koestler's words, 'unequal educational opportunities, placing privilege before merit, is the original sin which tears a nation apart and delivers it to the rule, not of a meritocracy, but of a mediocracy' (*DI*, p. 81).

That autumn, he submitted his new book *The Act of Creation* to the publishers. It was designed as a magnum opus, but when it appeared in May 1964 it had very mixed reviews, although it was more popular with younger people.[38] With over seven hundred pages, *The Act of Creation* is Koestler's longest book and would have benefited from a good editor. Frequently repetitive, it is ostensibly an intervention in the debate on the 'two cultures' to prove that there is substantial common ground between the humanities and the natural sciences. A less generous reading might call it a very lengthy attempt to demonstrate how useful Koestler's ideas about bisociation were and how they could be applied to processes of invention, innovation and discovery wherever they are found (in another context, Richard Freadman describes the 'somewhat homemade quality' of some of Koestler's conceptual work).[39] The volume is divided into two books, one looking at human creativity, the other at parallel structures in biology. At times insightful, at others tedious, it includes an astonishing breadth of examples encompassing the serious and the absurd, including such disparate topics as the ticklishness of gay men, the history of hand-washing in hospitals, the habits of singing magpies and the activities of rats in mazes.

At the heart of Koestler's theory of creativity in Book One, which is as much about scientific progress as it is about creativity in the artistic sense, is the idea that similar impulses lead to different results when expressed in the fields of comedy, science or the creative arts. Koestler admitted that this seemed like 'a basketful of wild generalizations', but it makes more sense in the context of Koestler's description of the extensive grey areas between the most objective and verifiable of the sciences (in his view, chemistry) and the most subjective or emotional of artistic disciplines (at least within literature, poetry). Medicine, psychology, anthropology, history, biography and the biographical novel, for example, are just progressive steps on a curve between two unreachable extremes: objectivity and subjective expression (AC, pp. 27–8; pp. 331–2).

Koestler lamented the 'two cultures' phenomenon, professing his incomprehension at the disdain of educated people towards scientific knowledge (AC, p. 264). Science and artistic production are seen by Koestler as parallel, connected activities, the differences between which have been exaggerated, one striving to discover a universal pattern, the other reaching back to archetype (AC, p. 353). He suggested that, like the arts, science should be seen in terms of genres and movements, and claimed that both were equally impressionistic in their representation of reality (AC, p. 252; p. 264). He contrasted the ways in which artists describe their working methods in rational terms, while scientists often emphasize their flashes of creative inspiration (AC, p. 329). Koestler thought that the argument was clinched by the philosophical problem of truth in science, that what is presented as evidence is only really an argument confirming or disproving a hypothesis, reiterating a point made previously by Karl Popper in *The Logic of Scientific Discovery* (1935).[40] Science is more like historiography than it seems, as it is a dynamic process of reformulating a view of the world based on new information and theories (*AC*, p. 242; p. 266).

Koestler's starting point in his account of creativity was laughter, as the only human reflex with no apparent use in evolutionary terms and one which demonstrated a physical response to mental stimulation. Koestler saw this as an exemplary form of bisociation and showed why he thought all jokes follow a similar logic (*AC*, p. 35). Associative thinking, making links between otherwise unconnected areas, was at the heart of not just humour, but science and the arts. Each discrete area to be connected with another was to be thought of as a 'matrix', which was governed by fixed rules or 'codes' (*AC*, pp. 38–40). One way of conceiving this, according to Koestler, was to think of a chess board. The board represents the matrix, while each chess piece is governed by a code. Bisociating between such matrices is a way of generating insights, making jokes and developing scientific and artistic innovations. One of the difficulties of this, however, is that many human codes, like riding a bike or tying up shoelaces, are subconscious. Koestler wished to show that creative thinking was dependent on the kinds of background, subconscious mental processes that let us ride a bike without thinking about how we are doing it (*AC*, pp. 42–4).

Associative thinking, however, seemed to be a sore point for Koestler. He was at pains to distinguish his concept of bisociation from that of associative thinking, suggesting that bisociation was the hallmark of creative originality, while associations were a habitual, everyday practice (*AC*, p. 647). According to Koestler, creative originality, whether in art or science, depends on two ideas from entirely different areas being brought together in productive synthesis, and a crucial part is played by the subconscious world of dream logic (*AC*, pp. 657–8). As such, dreams, hunches and instinctive conclusions are fundamental to Koestler's *The Act of Creation*, the title of which necessarily brings to mind Michelangelo's Sistine Chapel frescoes and the Genesis creation myths.

Many people come close to making big discoveries but do not make the necessary deductions at the right moment. Koestler dubbed this phenomenon 'snowblindness', a kind of typically human inability to see the obvious. He gave the example of Copernicus noticing, but not publishing, the elliptical shape of planetary orbits and Freud's early discovery of the anaesthetic properties of cocaine without considering how local anaesthetic might be useful in clinical practice (*AC*, pp. 217–19). Similarly, there have been many occasions where people have anticipated the solution of all the problems of science, only for a discovery to be made which turns everything on its head (*AC*, pp. 250–51). As described in *The Act of Creation*, the key to combatting snowblindness is interdisciplinarity, the unlikely pairings and cross-fertilizations between discourses, disciplines or intellectual traditions that lead to new discoveries (*AC*, p. 201; p. 230; p. 232). In Koestler's theory, though, interdisciplinarity on its own is not enough. A frequent misconception, according to Koestler, was that discoveries all come down from the brain functioning as a rational computer, but in fact many bubble up from the irrational and unpredictable workings of the unconscious (*AC*, p. 93; p. 157; p. 164; p. 211). Interdisciplinarity needs to be paired with openness towards unconscious intuition, as well as the willingness to break rules, to destroy as well as create, if rigid habits are to be overcome (*AC*, p. 104; p. 235; p. 334).

That originality is a form of rule breaking is paralleled in nature by the animal which changes the environment around it to achieve its own ends, or the combination of natural curiosity and daily uncertainty which is present in the natural world (*AC*, p. 448; p. 507). Koestler compared the dog that learns the signal for a mealtime to Kepler's noticing of a link between the movement of the moon and the pattern of the tides. Both the dog and the scientist have discovered that two events coincide, but neither can account for the reason why (*AC*, p. 589). This principle of contiguity, the noticing of apparent causal links between events, without real proof, is what drives the process of discovery. The skill, though, is not in asking *how* the two events are linked, but *why*; the great scientists rarely had the right answers to their problems, but simply asked the right questions (*AC*, p. 126).

Koestler was interested in the mystical elements of science that he had described in *The Sleepwalkers*. One of the important claims he makes is that 'Eureka moments' are chance events based on the activity of the unconscious mind, however much they depend on years of hard graft or meticulous benchwork. He makes a secondary claim that the great scientists often followed hunches or were motivated by aesthetic concerns that were sometimes at odds with the data they had: the problem of snowblindness in reverse. He lists examples of scientists who have described such mysterious processes of discovery, including Henri Poincaré, André-Marie Ampère and Karl Friedrich Gauss (*AC*, pp. 114–18). Koestler's favourite example, of course, was Johannes Kepler, who was still looking for perfect order in the universe when he was finally forced to accept that planetary orbits around the sun were roughly elliptical, and not circular as he had hitherto doggedly maintained (*AC*, p. 129).

Mysticism is in turn linked by Koestler to humour, for in jokes it is the magic element of the riddle that demands the participation of the listener, rehearsing the act of the joke's creation, just as when listening to a Christian parable the listener is required to search for the meaning of a story and re-create it (*AC*, p. 86; pp. 337–8). Koestler was also interested by the superstitious or religious belief in the power of etymology, the traces of ancient languages in contemporary vocabulary and other ideas about the magic powers of words (*AC*, pp. 186–7; pp. 312–15). Underlying rhythmic and rhymed word play, as well as the process of scientific discovery, is the notion of the pattern, apparently meaningful and coincidentally beautiful. From these creative patterns of humour and magical language, it is only a small step to the rational–irrational process of scientific discovery. Identifying three stereotypes of academics, the mad professor, the uninspired pedant and the benevolent magician, Koestler stated that it was the scientist-magician, such as Galileo, Newton or Einstein, who can be seen to integrate knowledge, motivated by 'a sense of power' and 'a sense of oceanic wonder'. The feeling of wonder was for Koestler, 'the common source of religious mysticism, of pure science and art for art's sake' (*AC*, pp. 255–8; pp. 262–3). He gave the example of Louis Pasteur, who late in life questioned scientific orthodoxy by speculating that one day life may be understood to have created matter, and not vice versa (*AC*, p. 702).

Book Two of *The Act of Creation* Koestler intended to be an account of the same territory within biological theory, but in fact it introduces few new ideas. One of the aspects that does come through more strongly in Book Two is the idea that evolution generates an excess of capability, which humans are still living up to. These mental capacities implied for Koestler that Stone Age man had, in principle, the mental ability to understand the construction of the atom bomb, and was evidence for him that Darwinian theory is not the final word in evolutionary theory (*AC*, p. 493). It was also an opportunity to expand on his ideas about a universal hierarchy, governed by matrices and codes, as well as the 'self-asserting' and 'participatory' tendencies (*AC*, p. 54; pp. 288–91; pp. 433–45; p. 488; p. 519; p. 526). Even for Koestler, though, there were limits to how far a theory of hierarchies could go, at least as far as human cultures were concerned, as the hundreds of abandoned movements, theories and ideologies bear witness to (*AC*, pp. 619–21).

As clearly limited as Koestler's ideas were, they should not be assessed for their ability to describe contemporary phenomena, or at least not only. It is also important to think of them as points of reference for his readers, creative impulses that caught the imagination, even of a much reduced readership from his *Darkness at Noon* heyday. One intriguing, and perhaps surprising possibility is the influence they may have had on the author Philip Roth. James Duban goes as far as to suggest that the literary implementation of Koestlerian 'bisociation' is a 'key component of Roth's artistry'.[41] He identifies elements of bisociation in the novels *Indignation* (2008) and *The Humbling* (2009) and the short story 'Eli, the Fanatic' (1959), also noting the connections between the latter text and Koestler's account of Palestine, *Promise and Fulfilment* (1949).[42] Inasmuch as Roth is one of the major American authors of the twentieth and twenty-first centuries, this influence suggests a lasting relevance for Koestler's ideas as having had a formative influence on cultural production in our time.

It is more difficult to assess the theoretical impact of Koestler's work, as it was closely bound up with that of other figures such as Polanyi or Ludwig von Bertalanffy. Investigating the reception of Koestler's work is also to ask the wrong question, for it is Koestler who was responsible for bringing the ideas of others to broader audiences. This is not to say that he made no impact in intellectual circles. Conversations with Polanyi in 1963 and 1964 led to the foundation of a 'Study Group on the Unity of Knowledge' and a symposium held at Bowdoin College, Maine, in 1965 – although, citing other engagements, Koestler did not attend.[43] In a talk on creativity and scientific progress, Polanyi referred to Koestler's *The Sleepwalkers* and mentioned the examples of Copernicus and Kepler. And, although he does not talk about *The Act of Creation*, the talk illustrates some of the ways in which Polanyi and Koestler found common ground. For example, Polanyi talked of 'the presence of the *promise* of coherence' as a factor guiding a scientist's intuition.[44]

Similarly, Manfred Drack and Wilfried Apfalter have tentatively defined a 'Vienna school' of system theory, represented by von Bertalanffy and Paul Weiss, but have disputed Koestler's place within it. Koestler, they suggest, was a popularizer, even though some of his ideas were welcomed by the systems theory field.[45]

6

Uncertain Evolution

What is one to make of an author whose creativity and enthusiasm are almost contagious, but whose attempts in the philosophy of science often come across as wooden and forced? One solution is to try to distinguish between Koestler's vision and its detail, as Henry Aiken suggested. As he put it, Koestler's work was 'truly creative' but his ideas appealed more to the emotions than to any empirical faculty; it formed 'not a thesis, but a vision, not a theory, but a unifying picture which, in an age of specialization, of bifurcations – and walls – is a refreshment of the soul'.[1] Aiken's warm endorsement of Koestler is about the best that can be said of his later work, which, for most impartial observers, was riddled with intellectual problems.

Personal problems were not far away, either. In the summer of 1964 Koestler was invited to spend time in Stanford. He felt obliged to take Cynthia with him. He was clearly still in love with Eva, but when he asked her for advice in Alpbach, she told him to marry Cynthia. Koestler struggled with the decision. He told Cynthia two days later that he was going to commit suicide, but she replied that if he did, then so would she. In the end he didn't follow through, and they were married in New York City Hall on 4 January 1965. It was more than ten years since Mamaine's death, and over fifteen years since Cynthia and Koestler first met. Koestler was 59, Cynthia was still just 38.

Koestler was a man entering the final phase of his career and was in search of an intellectual legacy. Acknowledgement and recognition were two things that, whether by accident or design, Koestler achieved very early in his career. Nevertheless, his fellowship in Stanford betrays his desire to be taken seriously as a theorist of science. He once told A. J. Ayer that he dreamed of being 'the Darwin of the twentieth century'.[2] He gave graduate seminars, as well as public lectures, in Stanford and Berkeley in 1965 and, when not in Palo Alto, he made trips with Cynthia to San Francisco, Monterey, Carmel and Big Sur. He also met Erik Erikson and Roman Jakobson, and planned to co-author a book on creativity with Karl Pribram.

As his stint in Stanford illustrates, Koestler was given high-profile platforms to explore his ideas, but perhaps not for the same reasons that he thought. He was a popularizer and an engaging speaker, invited by universities for his existing audience and his fame as much as for the originality of his insights. But even if he could not achieve real status in the academic world, he still possessed it in other ways. He remained very well-connected in literary and political circles and continued to live a cosmopolitan lifestyle. On their return to Europe in the summer of 1965, Koestler and Cynthia visited both Paris and Alpbach, meeting Manès Sperber, the publisher Robert Calmann-Lévy and the painter Françoise Gilot.

Koestler was given not only a platform, but forms of public recognition that marked him as having become part of the British establishment. That autumn, Koestler lectured in Cambridge and celebrated his sixtieth birthday.[3] To mark the occasion, the *Sunday Times* commissioned an interview with Koestler by Cyril Connolly in which they discussed a question that still dogs his work: was he a literary author or a journalist? It must have been a frustrating question for someone who was so eager to be seen as an intellectual, but public exposure did not liberate him from public scrutiny. If one were to speculate why the 'late', apparently naive Koestler seems so different to his earlier, Marxist self then this element of public non-recognition must also be taken into account. Did the fact that his books were being read by fewer and fewer people, and not even taken seriously by all of them, lead him into an intellectual corner where contrariness became a badge of honour?

At one level Koestler was trying to popularize the history of science; on another he was advocating interdisciplinarity. He was inspired by the idea of a universal web of knowledge and by what Goethe phrased as the 'imperative need to connect, only connect'.[4] Koestler's emphasis on the way many of the most important scientists in history were motivated by aesthetic ideas and by a sense of oceanic 'wonder' betrays this influence. In the age of Goethe the idea of the 'sublime' in nature became a main concern, an aesthetic and philosophical response to the sense of wonder. For Goethe, the mysteries of the natural world pointed to some kind of universal design.[5] As Scammell has noted, Koestler's 'wonder' did not extend to faith, and he 'steadfastly refused to believe in a personal god'.[6]

Koestler was becoming too steadfast in general. While staying with him in 1966, Polanyi found Koestler unwilling to concede any intellectual ground. Although the discussion was not futile, Polanyi wrote that Koestler 'has forgotten that one can contradict him'.[7] If Koestler was increasingly guilty of intellectual hubris it may have led to problems elsewhere in his life. Koestler was working in an age in which the sublime was out of fashion and, increasingly, so was he. With the project with Pribram now cancelled, Koestler lectured on evolution in Washington. He began working on a new book, which became *The Ghost in the Machine*, and spent the summer in Alpbach, but his relationship with Eva had cooled. That autumn, Koestler told Eva he was losing friends.[8]

Koestler's new book was an account of the hypothesis that man is a fundamentally flawed animal unlike any other in nature, prone to waging wars against other humans in support of religions, ideologies or national identities. Koestler advocated the development of a medicine that would counteract what he thought was an evolutionary aberration and what might otherwise be thought of as 'original sin'. On the basis that other artificial technologies from clothes to condoms have become indispensable elements of human life, Koestler thought that people would voluntarily opt to use medicine to gain control of their emotions. Technologies such as contraception, in his view, amounted to ways of compensating for evolutionary shortcomings. While he understood that biochemistry could be exploited by narrow interests groups against the majority, he did not think of this 'peace pill' as some kind of miracle cure, but as a drug that would have no noticeable effect, except to make the brain work in a more coordinated way.

His readers, or so he naively hoped, would understand what he was getting at (*GM*, pp. 327–9). Koestler's first official biographer certainly did not, writing 'I cannot think of any argument strong enough to support Koestler's Faustian plea for a cupful of transformation from some Mephistophelean alembic.'[9] Nevertheless, the idea caught the imagination of at least one world-famous writer when Agatha Christie reused the idea under the guise of 'Project Benvo' in one of her late novels, *Passenger to Frankfurt* (1970), a paranoid tale of a global Aryan conspiracy, though not one of her best books.[10] But *The Ghost in the Machine* is perhaps chiefly famous for having given the name to a 1981 album by The Police, the band of which Sting was the lead singer. One of the songs, 'Spirits in the Material World', was inspired by the idea of humanity being biologically predisposed to violence.

One of the reasons for Koestler's somewhat radical idea were his fears about the increasing unsustainability of human life. He strikes an alarmist tone when he talks of humanity now living in an 'age of climax', in which it accelerates to disaster (*GM*, pp. 315–27). Not only would the world population exceed planetary resources within a century, it also now possessed the military capability with nuclear and chemical weapons to effectively destroy itself and all that was good in the world (*GM*, p. 317). In Koestler's opinion, human wars, whether the Arab–Israeli conflict or the Cold War, needed to be resolved with no further delay if complete disaster was to be averted. At fault was humanity's 'schizophysiology', its Jekyll and Hyde nature derived from its evolutionary history, and a form of medication was the only answer.

Koestler's theory was based on the hierarchical theory of all knowledge that he had outlined in previous books. As before, Koestler drew heavily on the work of von Bertalanffy and his 'general systems theory', the attempt to create a universal theory of knowledge that could be applied across all disciplines. The idea behind the main metaphor of *The Ghost in the Machine*, which addresses the question as to why man can never really be thought of as an instinct-driven machine, is also derived from von Bertalanffy's work (*GM*, p. 109). Although Koestler was going back over ground he had covered in *The Act of Creation*, which discussed creativity and artistic and scientific achievement, *The Ghost in the Machine* was devoted to humanity's failings, not just in terms of future dystopian scenarios, but primarily as a question of the theory of the mind. In this sense, science could not offer a solution to the problem, but it could be used to determine which questions were the right ones to ask, as long as the cutting-edge of research in the life sciences was taken into account (*GM*, p. xiii).

The term 'ghost in the machine' itself was derived from Gilbert Ryle's 1949 book *The Concept of the Mind*, where it was used to draw critical attention to the way mental processes are often thought of as being somehow disconnected from physical ones. Koestler thought it important to concentrate on the mind, while also breaking down the 'mind-matter dichotomy' in favour of 'a multi-levelled hierarchy' (*GM*, p. 205). The decision-making mind sits at the top of this hierarchy, so complete awareness of it is always out of reach. Koestler's Janus-faced holons have a metaphorical role here, for if we look upwards in the open-ended hierarchy we perceive ourselves as free, but if we look down we see ourselves limited by animalistic and machine-like tendencies. Habit and uncontrollable passion were what Koestler saw as the true enemies of freedom (GM, p. 213; p. 217).

In *The Ghost in the Machine*, mankind is described as a very special kind of machine, namely one possessing a unique evolutionary aberration which means that it is able to constantly increase its intellectual capacities, because the human brain is capable of far more than we use it for. He used an analogy about an illiterate market trader given a hi-tech computer which he is wholly unable to use (GM, p. 298). Koestler thought that this was essentially a vindication of Goethe's natural philosophy and he compared Goethe's idea of the archetypal 'Urpflanze' with the idea that evolution is not a wholly random process. Essentially he was arguing for some kind of theory of intelligent design (GM, p. 139). The parallel development of marsupial and placental mammals into recognizably similar species, despite Australia's geographical isolation, was evidence for this (GM, p. 185). Remaining steadfastly resistant to conventional religious explanations, for Koestler there was no Creator in the sky dictating the evolution of animals; rather he believed that each organism gave itself purpose and only had a limited number of options in evolutionary terms (GM, pp. 152–6).

Koestler was also interested in the moral question of why human violence persists. He argued that human aggression had less to do with selfish self-assertion than with the longing to be sublimated into a larger group entity. War and organized violence, often motivated by a higher cause, were certainly responsible for greater loss of life than thieves and murderers. It was also for this reason that the pacifist movement had had so little success. Koestler argued that instead of addressing man's selfishness, we should instead concentrate on his selflessness (GM, pp. 233–4). Even twentieth-century history, to which Koestler was a witness, should not be divorced from the longer history of human violence, including ancient and tribal practices of human sacrifice. In the story of Abraham's willingness to kill his son Isaac, Koestler saw evidence for a congenital paranoia in humankind that was able to override even the evolutionary instinct for survival (*GM*, p. 239; p. 305). Here was the real ghost in the machine.

If this was the problem, what was the solution? One of Koestler's answers, a special pill that would help the brain overcome its evolutionary shortcomings, has already been given. *The Ghost in the Machine* also contains a second, more traditional answer. Koestler described the excessive identification with the mass group as a cheap way of finding meaning beyond oneself and he saw people's basic spiritual poverty as the thing to be addressed (*GM*, p. 248). It was transcendental beliefs that were lacking, especially among the educated elite, who placed too much faith in the explanatory powers of science, even though they did not understand the science themselves. This credulous world view was a sad and limited one for, as Koestler put it, it had 'no room for shadows, twilights and myths' (*GM*, p. 256).

The publication of *The Ghost in the Machine* in 1967 caused a small furore.[11] Stephen Toulmin pointed out that the book's diverse topics are only connected if you accept the highly problematic 'teleological interpretation of organic evolution' that Koestler puts forth. Of the peace pill, Toulmin also asked 'if there were such a pill: would Arthur Koestler take it?'[12] Given the kind of views that Koestler expressed in the book, events in the next few years of his life are revealing of the kind of person he was trying to be, and hoped to have become. Some details reveal the Koestler of old, such as when he was arrested for drink-driving in March 1967. His decision to withdraw from political journalism and activism illustrates how he deprived the world of a strident and independent opinion on Israel, particularly at the time of the Six Day War of 1967, which saw Israel occupy the Sinai Peninsula, the Gaza Strip, the West Bank and the Golan Heights.[13] It was a curious state of affairs for someone who, in his own way, was a kind of authoritative voice on the subject.

He ploughed on with the question of reductionism, organizing a symposium in Alpbach in 1968 titled 'Beyond Reductionism: New Perspectives in the Life Sciences'. Besides, it seemed as though his new career path was paying off. The same year saw Koestler awarded the Sonning Prize by the University of Copenhagen, which commends outstanding contributions to European culture. In recent years, recipients have included Michael Haneke and Orhan Pamuk, and it is interesting to note that Koestler was given the award before Hannah Arendt, Karl Popper or Simone de Beauvoir, who were all later recipients. Also in 1968, Queen's University in Canada awarded him an honorary doctorate and he took the opportunity presented by the acceptance speech to talk about the student protest movement. A year later in 1969, Koestler had hopes of being awarded the Nobel Prize in Literature, the one achievement which could have cemented his reputation. He was disappointed when it was given to Samuel Beckett, a man seven months his junior. Beckett was similarly connected to France and the Continent, but his life and works were very different to Koestler's own.

Koestler seemed to be losing his touch. He had ended 1968 with a disastrous trip to Australia, where he was subject to hostile press coverage (Joseph Strelka has speculated that Soviet secret service interference may even have been to blame for this).[14] He continued to court controversy on the subject of drugs. And he took the opportunity to publish a provocative short story about Christ called 'The Misunderstanding' (later published in Britain as 'Episode').[15]

The following year Koestler considered writing a new volume of autobiography, but in the end decided not to. This decision proved to be a fateful one, for Koestler's life is exciting and action-packed as long as he describes it, and more difficult to follow where his autobiographical narration gives out. He had multiple reasons not to write it. Despite outward success as a writer of non-fiction, he must have sensed that he was not quite the 'real deal'. Would a third autobiography have been the story of the man he no longer was, or the story of the man he wished he could have been?

Traces of both the man Koestler was and the one he wanted to become can be seen in the interdisciplinary symposium 'Beyond Reductionism' that Koestler organized in Alpbach in 1968. It featured a range of high-profile intellectuals from top universities in Europe and the USA, including other prominent Austrians or former Austrians such as Paul Weiss, Ludwig von Bertalanffy, Friedrich Hayek and Viktor Frankl, who were all the same age or slightly older than Koestler. They were the kind of people who had much in common with him. Hayek had been working in America and Britain prior to the Nazi dictatorship and chose to remain in Britain during the war, publishing his book *The Road to Serfdom* in 1944. Like Koestler's *Darkness at Noon*, it has been seen as an anti-totalitarian and not simply anti-Communist work. Frankl was only five months older than Koestler and had achieved prominence with a 1946 book on his experiences in the concentration camps, published in English as *Man's Search for Meaning*. The symposium also featured prominent American academics such as Jerome Bruner, Paul D. MacLean, David McNeill and Seymour S. Kety, as well as the Swiss psychologist Jean Piaget and the British biologist C. H. Waddington. The topics discussed were diverse, covering evolution, psychopharmacology, the theory of knowledge, biochemistry, and free will and determinism, as well as Koestler's notion of the holon.

The image of Koestler at this time is of a man at the last peak of his career, still active as an author, perhaps still searching for a legacy. He was a sought-after public speaker, the kind he would later describe as 'call girls'. Alongside figures such as E. H. Gombrich, W. H. Auden and Margaret Mead, Koestler spoke at the

1969 Nobel Symposium in Stockholm on the topic of reductionism in Western education, arguing against 'nothing-but-ism' and a theory of evolution based on 'random mutations', which he compared to painters throwing 'fistfuls of paint at the canvas'. He argued that one of the achievements of the 1968 generation was to draw attention to the crisis of meaning that dogs modern societies, which was also a crisis of education.[16] In a second talk, he revisited the topics he covered in *The Ghost in the Machine*, arguing that mankind has a destructive streak and, contrary to popular belief, was not too selfish, but rather too devoted to violent common causes.[17]

Even as he continued to enjoy a widespread recognition, he clearly also began to consider the subject of his own death. In 1969 he joined the Voluntary Euthanasia Society, having taken an interest in bids to legalize assisted dying that year, later becoming the society's Vice-President. Assisted Dying had been the subject of a private member's bill in Parliament, the Voluntary Euthanasia Bill of 1969, which was described by its proposer Lord Raglan as 'a liberal and humanitarian measure for those who treasure for themselves the quality of life as much as its quantity'.[18]

In 1970 Koestler began working on *The Case of the Midwife Toad*, a study of the life and work of Paul Kammerer, framed as an investigative quest for the truth. Kammerer (1880–1926) was an Austrian biologist whose reputation was ruined after it was insinuated that he had doctored a toad specimen with ink in a desperate bid to provide evidence for the theory of acquired characteristics in evolution. Despite the offer of a professorship in Moscow, Kammerer killed himself a number of weeks after the allegation was made. The suicide seemed to many like an admission of guilt, but Koestler lists a series of alternative reasons for it, as well as casting doubt on the theory that Kammerer faked his results.

Koestler found Kammerer's work exciting and even inspiring. He set out to find out more about him and ended up attempting to rehabilitate Kammerer's reputation. *The Case of the Midwife Toad* portrays the life story of a gifted but unlucky man who was tragically misunderstood and who was used as cannon fodder for the dogmatic interests of his international biologist colleagues. Kammerer had originally intended to become a musician, but had later opted for science. He had a particular talent for breeding lizards, among other creatures, and was employed by Professor Hans Przibram to work at his Institute for Experimental Biology in Vienna. Before the First World War, Kammerer's reputation was largely intact. He had published over two hundred pages of scientific notes over a period of fourteen years detailing ground-breaking experiments on the adaptive capabilities of salamanders and toads. He believed that he had found evidence that Lamarck's critique of Darwinian evolutionary theory was at least partially correct, as his experiments showed that certain breeds of salamander and toad developed adaptive capabilities when kept in controlled conditions for a number of generations. This seemed to imply that evolution was not merely random, but depended on the inheritance of adapted characteristics.

Koestler kept an open mind on the question of Lamarck but defended Kammerer's work on the basis that plenty of scientists are able to fully explain their results at the time they obtain them. Kammerer had been able to obtain colour changes in salamanders and, by making land-loving toads mate in water, he was able to obtain developmental features otherwise only known in the breed's more aquatic cousins. The results of Kammerer's experiments were radical but they were tricky to repeat, especially given the state and cost of lab technology at the time. Koestler laments at regular intervals that no one has ever repeated Kammerer's experiments to see if they were correct (*MT*, p. 100). Kammerer also experimented on sea squirts and newts and claimed to have restored the sight of an olm (*Proteus anguinus*), an otherwise blind, cave-dwelling salamander species, by raising it in red light.

It was the experiments on the so-called 'midwife toad' that were to prove crucial. As Koestler shows convincingly in the book, Kammerer did not find these results conclusive, but he was forced to defend them against aggressive criticism by an English biologist named William Bateson. Bateson, who was notable for pioneering the use of the term 'genetics' in a biological context, had a grudge against Lamarckism, having failed to find evidence for it after more than a year's fieldwork in Central Asia. His son later told Koestler that his father had regarded Lamarckism thereafter as a 'tabooed pot of jam to which he was not allowed to reach' (*MT*, p. 51). As Koestler showed, Bateson clearly wanted to extend the taboo to others.

Things began to go wrong for Kammerer, scientifically speaking, when Bateson requested material evidence of his claims about the midwife toads. Kammerer sent a confusing reply, which later led Bateson to believe that Kammerer had something to hide. In Koestler's view, Kammerer was unable to send Bateson a sample at that time as his toads were still alive and not currently mating. In addition, Bateson did not make his hostile intent clear to Kammerer, who could have been forgiven for thinking Bateson was genuinely interested in his work. Even without seeing a specimen, Bateson told his wife that he wanted to prove Kammerer wrong (*MT*, pp. 60–63). His approach was anything but open-minded. When, in 1923, Kammerer travelled to Cambridge to give a lecture and demonstrate his specimens, Bateson declined to attend, even though the talk had been organized by his son. And, when he attended Kammerer's lecture at the Linnean Society in London, he did not examine the specimens in any detail, even though this had been his long-standing wish. In a breathtakingly manipulative act, he then requested to see the specimen after Kammerer had returned to Austria. Understandably frustrated, both Kammerer and the director of the Vienna institute, Hans Przibram, declined Bateson's request.

Paul Kammerer, the controversial Austrian biologist and inspiration for *The Case of the Midwife Toad*.

Although none of the biologists who did see Kammerer's specimens in Austria or England raised any doubt about their authenticity on inspecting them, a real scandal broke out when an American named G. K. Noble inspected a specimen of Kammerer's toads in Vienna in 1926. Working with another biologist, Paul Weiss (later a friend of Koestler's), Noble proved that supposedly characteristic black markings on the toad had been created by injecting black ink into the specimen. He published news of the fake in the journal *Nature* that summer, an event which was widely seen as precipitating Kammerer's suicide only six weeks later.

Koestler did not believe that a forgery so easily discovered could have fooled a whole series of eminent biologists in Vienna, London and Cambridge. He speculated about the motives of a person who could have sabotaged Kammerer, or why Kammerer might himself have doctored the specimen. He also sought to dissociate the suicide from the accusations of scientific fraud, showing that Kammerer gave a whole series of different reasons for his decision, only one of which related to the toad specimen. He had been in love with the famous dancer Grete Wiesenthal, but she had refused to travel with him to Moscow. He had bipolar tendencies, and had suffered both financial ruin and the loss of his collection of specimens in the fallout of the First World War. In short, Koestler judged Kammerer to have been the victim of a situation over which he felt he had little control, with multiple motives for suicide. After Kammerer's death, few people attempted to defend his scientific reputation (*MT*, p. 102).

Koestler argued that, as the experiments have never been repeated, no one had actually proven Kammerer wrong, and he believed that his account of the affair showed that revisiting Kammerer's work could be worthwhile (*MT*, p. 103, p. 174). He judged it unlikely that multiple members of the Vienna laboratory had conspired to fake Kammerer's results. Koestler's hypothesis was that the specimen had been tampered with shortly before Noble's visit to Vienna, perhaps only a few days before. Whether it was Kammerer himself who did the tampering, or a colleague with well-meant or even malign intentions, was a question that Koestler left open. His personal view was that Kammerer was not stupid enough to inject ink into a specimen knowing that it would be inspected by expert biologists, and that he was in any case no longer working at the institute (*MT*, pp. 107–9).

Crucial evidence was provided by Paul Weiss, the same man who participated at the Alpbach symposium, who stated that dark fluid flowed out of the specimen on dissection. During the writing of *The Case of the Midwife Toad*, Koestler took the unprecedented step of asking Holger Hydén of the University of Gothenburg, another Alpbach delegate, to repeat Kammerer's alleged forgery.

The results Hydén obtained showed that ink rapidly faded or dissolved when injected in the specimens, regardless of whether they were preserved in alcohol or formaldehyde, and congealed when fixed using gelatine (*MT*, pp. 109–13). In order for the ink to flow out of the specimen, it would have had to have been recently injected. The director of the laboratory, Hans Przibram, also thought there had been a set-up. He told his brother that he thought he knew who had done the tampering, but did not have enough evidence to accuse them. Koestler speculated about anti-Communist political motives, which, given that Kammerer was about to emigrate to the Soviet Union, could not be excluded. Weight was lent to this theory by the fact that, despite Kammerer's reputation being in tatters, his invitation to Moscow was not withdrawn. For what it was worth, a political motive was also given in a Soviet film based on Kammerer's life, titled *Salamandra* (1928) (*MT*, pp. 115–16).

The circumstances of Kammerer's suicide were also suitably dramatic. He travelled to the Schneeberg, a mountain in Lower Austria, and shot himself. He chose a difficult method, holding the gun with his right hand to the left side of his head. He wrote four letters as suicide notes, and gave at least three different reasons for his decision. He told the Moscow Academy of Science that he considered his life's work to have been destroyed; he told his ex-wife Felicitas von Wiedersperg that he could not bear to leave Vienna; and gave further undisclosed reasons to one of his friends as well as to Grete Wiesenthal. Koestler wrote that Kammerer's death 'had a touch of melodrama, but so had his life. He was a Byron among the toads' (*MT*, pp. 117–21).

Writing Kammerer's life was for Koestler to some degree a form of 'displaced autobiography'. Kammerer was a misunderstood scientist from Vienna who saw significance in coincidences, distrusted the prevailing theories of evolution and developed a sideline in journalism.[19] It can also be seen as part of collective activity. Literary production by former Austrian and German political exiles was highly diverse, but it is worth noting that several of those active in journalism in London during the war later chose to write biographies of German or Austrian cultural figures. Such biographies can perhaps be seen as forms of reconciliation between or reappropriation of the biographers' respective cultures. Examples include Carl Brinitzer's 1960 'novel' of Heinrich Heine's life, Hilde Spiel's 1962 account of Fanny von Arnstein and Robert Lucas's 1972 study of the relationship between Frieda von Richthofen and D. H. Lawrence.[20]

Koestler also tried to live up to Kammerer's example (imitation being the highest form of biographical compliment). Inspired by Kammerer's work *Das Gesetz der Serie* (The Law of the Series, 1919), Cynthia and Arthur began collecting accounts of coincidences. Koestler had relegated Kammerer's work on coincidences to an appendix of *The Case of the Midwife Toad*, but marvelled over the chance that on the same day that he learnt from two separate sources about Kammerer's affair with Grete Wiesenthal, the woman herself died. Kammerer had theorized that coincidence is a universal principle in nature which is insufficiently understood, although, no doubt to Koestler's disappointment, Kammerer had discounted all kinds of parapsychological explanation (*MT*, pp. 137–8; p. 143). It was this project that would lead to Koestler's next book, *The Roots of Coincidence*.

In the early 1970s, Koestler was by no means forgotten, even if his star was definitely on the wane. At the end of 1971, Koestler learned that he would be honoured with a CBE in the New Year's Honours list for 1972. In the list his occupation was categorized as 'Author' (and not 'Journalist' as some would still have it). Perhaps more gratifyingly, at the very end of 1969, the final abolition of hanging in the United Kingdom was approved by Parliament, making permanent a suspension of capital punishment that had been effective since 1965. This came as a belated reward for Koestler's efforts (as well as Cynthia's) in the 1950s. Coming alongside movements for reform on issues such as abortion, euthanasia and suicide, it was part of a cultural shift in British attitudes on the question of death.[21]

In 1970 Cynthia also learnt the terrible truth about her father's death: he had been a heroin addict and had cut his wrists open in the bath.[22] Cynthia is ever the shadow in biographies of Koestler and the hushed-up tragedy in her childhood is a detail that perhaps helps explain why she was able to put up with a position in Koestler's life that others would have found intolerable. The new (and no doubt deeply shocking) information about her past coincided with another shift in her life with Koestler. With Koestler nearing his 65th birthday, the couple finally began to settle down. They bought a house in Denston in Suffolk, which, together with the London flat, would be their final home. The Alpbach house was sold the following year and, as if to commemorate his time there, Koestler began working on a novel about a high-profile academic conference in a fictive mountain village, published as *The Call Girls* in 1972. While Cynthia and Arthur were by no means always a happy couple, their departure from Alpbach meant that Koestler's relationship with Eva Auer was effectively over.[23]

The Roots of Coincidence was published in early 1972. A relatively short work with only 140 pages, it was a sequel to *The Case of the Midwife Toad* but with the programmatic character of *The Act of Creation* and *The Ghost in the Machine* rather than the investigative quality of *The Case of the Midwife Toad* or the later *The Thirteenth Tribe*. It is on the whole an unconvincing book, covering topics such as telepathy and hypnosis, with the difficult goal of trying to convince readers that research into extrasensory perception was not only worthwhile, but could even be the future of psychology and physics. Koestler did not see any contradiction in working first on Kepler and the admirable empiricism of the scientific greats and then shifting to something as subjective as parapsychology. It was precisely the uncanny aspect of scientific discovery that he had touched on in *The Act of Creation* which was his ongoing concern. Was it possible, he speculated, that the brain is constantly filtering out extrasensory information, which only sometimes manages to break through? (*RC*, p. 131). In the fourth chapter of the book, Koestler also explains how parapsychology fits into his theory of 'Janus-faced holons', making *The Roots of Coincidence* a further iteration of Koestler's theory of everything, his attempt to universalize, to make a decisive contribution to knowledge. It was a typically futile gesture of his later work. Even Renée Haynes, the author of a postscript to the book, did not subscribe to Koestler's co-opting of parapsychology into his ideas about the oceanic feeling of being subsumed into infinity. She wrote, 'I must take issue with Mr Koestler . . . There can be no perception without a perceiver; and contemplatives retain their selves enough to perceive as they rejoice' (*RC*, pp. 148–9).

When it appeared, *The Call Girls* (1972) did not become a big success. It was an indulgent, even narcissistic novel that was effectively a rehashing of Koestler's ideas on the history of science, parapsychology and the peace pill in narrative form. It follows the progress of an academic conference attended by public intellectuals, the academic 'call girls' of the book's title, taking place in a thinly disguised version of Alpbach. It could be seen as a form of wish-fulfilment on Koestler's part, showing the kind of discussion of his ideas that he would have liked to have seen, with telegrams from the U.S. president and earnest discussions of Koestlerian topics. To some extent the book is capable of irony, as the figure most like Koestler, who is called Solovief, is portrayed as an ageing, terminally ill guru who has a bold plan to save humanity by introducing pacifist medication into the water supply. Yet even the self-ironizing elements are somewhat immodest in the sense that Solovief is a misunderstood visionary who (the reader may reasonably assume) shares the metaphysical insight of the protagonists of the novel's prologue and epilogue: a disillusioned Christ at Calvary and a paranoid delusionary at a psychiatric clinic.

The book's portrayal of women is almost undeniably sexist. The female characters are mostly dowdy and tedious wives, or big-busted, sexually available locals. Later, a bitter old spinster becomes pathologically violent and burns all the recordings of the conference, while the only real female intellectual figure, Harriet, is insecure about her looks as an older woman and has a fling with the caretaker. An implied lesbian encounter with one of the other guests ensues. Needless to say, women mostly talk to each other about men, rather than intellectual topics. The book's token gay character, 'Blood', is portrayed as overbearing and sinister, but is just about witty enough to be tolerated by the others. Overall, the tone of Koestler's attempted skit on academic life is aspirational rather than critical, and the characters and goings-on are too clichéd to be funny.

In the autumn of 1972, Janine, now Janine Greville, gave Koestler the opportunity to meet his daughter, who was already seventeen years old. Once again, he did not go through with it. On being told that Cristina had guessed her real father's identity, Koestler wrote to her to explain why he did not wish to meet her. She did not reply and later chose to disbelieve her mother's account. It is easy to understand why. From her perspective, it must be confusing to be written about in biographies in connection with a man you never met, let alone had a father–daughter relationship with, and who had effectively disowned you from the start. From a biographer's point of view, it is yet another moment in Koestler's life where he appears more than mildly unsympathetic. Family values, even disputed ones, were clearly not high on the Koestlerian agenda.

In 1973 the writer Iain Hamilton began writing a biography of Koestler, which George Mikes later termed the 'last great annoyance of his life'.[24] Koestler's decision to encourage and collaborate on the writing of his biography is in itself an interesting one. It was of course a 'self-promoting' decision, but it was also a marked contrast to George Orwell's futile attempt to prevent the writing of a biography about him. Orwell wanted to preserve his own carefully constructed self-image beyond his death.[25] Koestler threw caution to the wind and as Hamilton was sceptical about all of Koestler's later work, his book was by no means entirely complimentary. In a way this is revealing of a softer side of Koestler's nature. Many of his actions in his life may seem cruel on a personal level, or even criminal, in the case of the posthumous rape claim made against him. But there is every reason to believe that Koestler was a sincere if highly impulsive person, an engaging speaker with an extraordinary life, if ultimately not a philosophical genius. Collaborating with a biographer may be narcissistic, but it is less so than a ghostwritten autobiography would have been.

In 1974 Koestler observed Uri Geller's experiments, which led to a somewhat farcical episode. Geller was at the height of his fame owing to his apparently psychic spoon-bending abilities. The shadow of doubt that Geller was able so skilfully to create was precisely the kind of thing which interested Koestler. At the beginning of August Koestler resigned from the Council of the Society for Psychical Research, but over the summer he corresponded with J. B. Rhine on the question of Geller's authenticity. Koestler was impressed by Geller's skills and at the beginning of August Koestler had told Rhine that Geller was '50 per cent genuine'. Despite the scepticism of J. B. Hasted, who told the journals *Nature* and *Physics Today* not to publish the report of the test of Geller's abilities on the basis that it was insubstantial, Koestler was sounding almost confident by September, writing: 'I no longer have any doubt that at least some of the phenomena he produces when he has a good day are genuine (which does not exclude a little cheating on a bad day).'[26]

Gradually Koestler began to leave the topic behind, his book on telepathy with Alister Hardy and Robert Harvie, titled *The Challenge of Chance*, having been completed at the end of 1973. But even if Koestler's willingness to believe in the power of the mind to bend spoons makes him seem gullible, perhaps disappointingly so, it may be premature to write off Koestler's sideline in parapsychology. Reviewing Michael Scammell's biography in 2010, Neil Ascherson warned that writing off Koestler's later work 'could be a mistake'.[27] The reason was that Koestler's belief that science would ultimately discover phenomena that had previously been considered impossible could well be proven right; we are simply not able to say. But in 1974 *The Challenge of Chance* was poorly received. The renowned critic Brigid Brophy deemed it 'a classic among non-contributions to knowledge' and voiced her suspicion that an experiment described was not properly set up.[28] This largely concurs with George Mikes's own layman's view that Koestler had been tempted to 'combine fairytales with scientific proof, mystical balderdash with macro-physics'.[29]

Around 1974 Koestler also started working on the Khazar myth of Jewish origins, his final major project, and one entirely unrelated to the history (or, indeed, future) of science. It could be seen as a return to one of the other major topics of his youth: the political and cultural dilemmas of being Jewish. Early that same year Koestler also revisited the site of the former camp at Le Vernet, as well as Biarritz and Bayonne. He was also made a Companion of the UK's Royal Society of Literature. The following year, 1975, Koestler turned seventy and a Festschrift was organized for the occasion. It focused largely on his science and non-fiction writing and was titled *Astride the Two Cultures*.[30] In April the Hungarian exile and author Julius Hay, a friend of many years whose autobiography had recently appeared in English, wrote to Koestler from Switzerland for the last time before his death. In Hungarian, he wished Koestler all the best for the future and thanked him for a valued friendship.[31]

The publication of Koestler's *The Thirteenth Tribe: The Khazar Empire and its Heritage* followed in 1976. It became a *succès de scandale*, and bucked the trend of declining sales of Koestler's books.[32] Like *The Case of the Midwife Toad*, the book was written as an investigation into the truth of a dubious historical episode and ended with Koestler endorsing a potential hoax. Yet the success of *The Thirteenth Tribe* was deserved, for it reveals a fascinating story that most readers would have known next to nothing about. It details the story of the Khazar people, who in the first millennium AD were one of the dominant groups in Central Asia and the Caucasus. Their language was Turkic in origin and they fought for influence against the two major powers of the age: the Umayyad Caliphate and the Byzantine Empire. Although they were not a Semitic people, the Khazars converted to Judaism, presumably for strategic reasons. After enjoying centuries of dominance, they rapidly fell from power under pressure from the Mongol hordes, and promptly disappeared.

Koestler supported the theory that the Khazar people, like the Hungarians and Bulgarians, migrated to Central and Eastern Europe around the end of the first millennium. Around the same time, a significant Jewish population was established across Eastern Europe. Connecting the two historical facts seemed like the most simple explanation for this near simultaneous disappearance and emergence. Koestler also thought that Khazar heritage could explain the origins of the unique *shtetl* Jewish farming communities (*TT*, pp. 154–5). One problem with his theory, of course, was a lack of proof, but the real issue was the fact that the Khazar theory blew the story of Jewish exceptionalism and return to the promised land to smithereens. If it were correct, the majority of Jews alive in the world today would be more closely related to the Ottomans than to Moses, for the majority trace their ancestry to Eastern Europe and thus to the Khazars.

Koestler knew that his book would be dynamite in the wrong hands (as the numerous conspiracy videos about *The Thirteenth*

Tribe on YouTube demonstrate). Personally he thought the story of the Khazars pointed towards a 'cruel hoax', as it rendered the history of anti-Semitism meaningless (*TT*, p. 17). To this end he concluded the book with a defence of the right of Israel to exist and repeated his unfashionable view that Israel is a nation, but the Jewish people are not. He suggested again that Jewish people should either move to Israel or assimilate to the countries in which they live (*TT*, pp. 223–36). Koestler's rather anti-pluralist position on this question did not, in his opinion, have anything to do with Khazar history. Koestler would have vehemently rejected Leon Wieseltier's claim that 'only a Jew would have taken so much trouble to come up with an alibi for his own self-effacement.'[33] Others, like Buckard, have defended him. For Buckard, Koestler's own Jewishness is irrelevant because the book does not need to be seen as a rejection of his Jewish heritage.[34]

Koestler's account of the Khazar story begins around AD 740 as the Khazars were successful in halting the Muslim conquest of the northern Caucasus. That the Khazars converted to Judaism thereafter is not a matter of historical dispute, however unlikely it may seem to the Western reader encountering the story for the first time. As Koestler writes, the dispute is over what happened to the Jewish Khazars later, after their power had waned. Koestler was convinced that the majority emigrated to what is today Russia and Poland (and, presumably, Belarus). He even thought that the entry in the *Encylopaedia Judaica* admitted as much, for it talks of 'evidence attesting to the continued presence in Europe of descendants of the Khazars' (*TT*, pp. 15–16). The entry, written by Douglas Morton Dunlop (and, according to Koestler, amended by the editors), was based on Dunlop's 1954 book *History of the Jewish Khazars*. In the 2007 version of the encyclopaedia the entry remains unchanged.

The history of the Khazars has proven resistant to historical and archaeological research. The archaeological sites that relate

to them are located in Russia. One of them, Sarkel, is now
flooded by the Tsimliansk Reservoir on the Don River. Another,
Samandar, is thought to be located on the Terek river in the border
region between the troubled Russian territories of Chechnya
and Dagestan. Despite valiant efforts by Mikhail Artamonov to
decipher the Khazar past, the history of the Khazars was apparently
a threat to the ethnocentric narrative of Soviet Russia and
Artamonov's work was discredited. Koestler therefore suspected
political motives behind Artamonov's later denial of any Khazar
influence on Russian culture (*TT*, pp. 93–4). Khazar studies may
therefore have fallen victim to Soviet politics of memory – at
least for a time. Since the end of the Soviet Union, work on
potential 'Khazar' sites has resumed. The Russian archaeologist
Dmitrii Vasil'ev has suggested that the eighth- to tenth-century
layer of an excavation at the Samosdelka site in Russia's Astrakhan
region, ongoing since the 2000s, could correspond to the Khazar
capital of Itil. However, as he points out, it is ultimately impossible
to confirm the theory, despite suggestive pieces of evidence.[35]

Although Dunlop's entry in the *Encyclopaedia Judaica* claims
that Khazar Judaism was 'never very strong', Koestler maintained
that the disputed 'Khazar Correspondence' evidences that the
Jewish religion took root among the Khazar population and
they continued to practise it after migrating to Europe (*TT*,
pp. 73–4). Some of the Khazars moved westwards to Central
Europe at the end of the ninth century AD with the Magyars,
and the Khazar language was apparently spoken in Hungary
until the tenth century (*TT*, p. 100). The decline of the Khazars
in their homeland was precipitated, according to Koestler,
by the rise of Russia and specifically by Prince Vladimir's
conversion to Christianity in the years leading up to AD 990,
for it was at this point that the Khazar alliance with Byzantium
wore thin (*TT*, p. 126). They survived with less influence until the
thirteenth century, when their lands were overrun by the Mongol

hordes, causing their migration westwards into Eastern Europe (*TT*, p. 141).

Like any good conspiracy theory, much of Koestler's account is based on speculation, which gradually shifts into certainty. Khazars *may* have been invited to settle in Hungary by Duke Taksony, and they *may* have continued to practise their Jewish religion. They *may* have participated in the Magyar occupation of present-day Austria in the tenth century, which *may* in turn have led to a folk memory of a dynasty of Jewish princes ruling in the Vienna area (*TT*, pp. 100–101; p. 105; pp. 170–72). Koestler lists many other alleged influences. The Khazars *could* also have influenced a system of dual kingship in Hungary prior to St Stephen's turn to faith and his concentration of power in Hungary. The fact that Seljuk, the ancestor of the Seljuk dynasty, gave his sons Old Testament names *could* be because he grew up at the Khazar court. The threatening 'Red Jews' of old German folk tales *may* have referred to the Khazars. Koestler also claims a Khazarian origin for the tale of David Alroy's crusade from Kurdistan to Jerusalem, which *may* have given rise to the Star of David symbol, and which was reworked by Benjamin Disraeli in his novel *Alroy* (1833) (*TT*, pp. 133–7). Numerous old place names in the Ukraine, Poland and Austria *could* also be linked to the Khazars (*TT*, p. 145). In order to counteract the amount of the story which is based on such speculative claims, the later chapters of Koestler's book are characterized by statements of certainty; Koestler uses phrases such as 'the conclusion seems self-evident', 'established beyond dispute', 'we may safely conclude' or 'a strong case in favour' in order to eliminate doubt about the historical facts (*TT*, p. 152; p. 159; p. 168; p. 179).

Koestler's interest in links between the Khazars and the Jewish people may have been linked to the Hungarian nationalism of his youth, which drew on the Hungarian people's Central Asian heritage.[36] David Cesarani is sceptical about this link, as he sees

Koestler's Hungarian nationalism as taking place in spite of his Jewishness.[37] The American historian Derek Penslar, writing on a more recent attempt at debunking essentialist narratives of Jewish identity, Shlomo Sand's *The Invention of the Jewish People* (2008), describes it as a 'new anti-history, a counter-mythology that may hold enduring appeal to a world bemused by Israel ... and searching desperately for answers in the past, even one that never was'. He sees Koestler as one of Sand's predecessors, and the term 'counter-mythology' might also be applied to *The Thirteenth Tribe* too, for, like Sand, Koestler is really arguing that 'Jews comprise a religious civilization, not a people.' Undoubtedly, Koestler too taps into the logic of the conspiracy theory, which 'appeals precisely to people who see the Zionist project as a monumental exercise of bad faith'.[38] It would be unfair to say he did this for personal, political advantage. As Strelka has argued, the book can be seen as evidence of Koestler's commitment to identifying unpopular truths (even if he may have failed).[39] He did not use the theory of the Khazar origins of European Jews to try to delegitimize the state of Israel, seeing the two issues as unrelated, and in Koestler's favour, it can be said that the 'minimal' theory of a small Khazarian influence in the genetic history of European Jews is generally accepted.[40]

Its successor two years later was a retrospective of Koestler's works, titled *Janus: A Summing Up* (1978). This book was an attempt to synthesize and contextualize Koestler's thought as it had developed since the 1950s. It is a book with an extraordinary range which nevertheless makes clear which ideas it is most heavily invested in. These include von Bertalanffy's 'General Systems Theory'; Lamarckian notions of acquired characteristics, particularly as advocated by Kammerer; and the work of Karl Popper and Michael Polanyi. At various points, Koestler also referred to the work of the French biologist and Lamarckian Pierre-Paul Grassé, who believed that when the limitations of biological study were reached, it 'must hand over to metaphysics' (*J*, p. 226).

In 1979 Koestler was contacted by an editor at the University of California Press asking him if he would be interested in writing a book on homosexuality as a way of developing or going beyond simple 'nature or nurture' debates. Koestler declined the invitation briskly, stating that he had nothing to say on the matter. It was a subject that had previously interested him, though. He had taken a political interest in the subject as long ago as 1956, when he had accepted an invitation to the *Observer* offices to discuss proposals by the British Social Biology Council.[41] And Koestler did write about male homosexuality earlier in his career, albeit in a somewhat ambiguous way. The account in *L'Encyclopédie de la vie sexuelle*, co-written by Koestler with Willy Aldor and Ludwig Levy-Lenz (a former employee of Magnus Hirschfeld's Berlin Institut für Sexualwissenschaft), described the history of male homosexuality, as well as famous instances of it. Although largely non-judgemental of famous homosexuals in history, the account was included in a chapter titled 'Deviations of Object' that termed homosexuality 'abnormal' and a 'perversion', and also discussed transvestism, gerontophilia and necrophilia.[42] Written around the same time was Koestler's depiction of Roman sexual behaviour in *The Gladiators*, which included his casting of Spartacus's gladiatorial rival Crixus as bisexual, as well as the symbolic sexual exploitation of a returned slave by his Roman master. Later, Koestler made the unlikely claim in *Arrow in the Blue* that the free morals of Viennese working-class girls meant that homosexuality was never an issue in the student fraternities (*G*, p. 112; p. 310; *AB*, p. 91). Later still, in *The Sleepwalkers*, Koestler claimed that the history of science owes a debt to gay and bisexual people, as they 'have always proved to be the most devoted teachers and disciples' (itself a repetition of an idea that appears in the *Encyclopédie*) (*SW*, p. 154). While David Cesarani judged Koestler to have been homophobic, the balance of evidence does not support this view; Koestler appears to have been fairly ambivalent.[43] Oddly, too, Koestler used the word 'homophobia' in *The Lotus and the Robot* in a way that became obsolete not long afterwards, describing a fear of men or other people, rather than of gay men and women (*LR*, p. 213).

In later years, Koestler saw more of Mamaine's sister, Celia Goodman, as well as Daphne Hardy Henrion, his girlfriend of the late 1930s, who were both living nearby in East Anglia. Daphne completed a bust of Koestler, a copy of which is at the National Portrait Gallery in London, subsequently described as 'one of the most acute and moving portrait sculptures'.[44] Koestler also kept a framed photograph of Mamaine on his study wall, a sign of his ongoing sense of loss.[45] Among Koestler's friends was the literary critic George Steiner who, although 24 years his junior, shared some of Koestler's connections to the European Continent. Koestler and Steiner used to play chess together, as did Koestler and Julian Barnes when the latter visited in 1981.[46] Barnes, now a Booker Prize winner, had then recently published his first novel, *Metroland* (1980).

Despite his ailing health, Koestler continued to support causes new and old. He became patron of the London-based Institute for UFO Studies in March 1980, although he never played an active role. The Institute promised to study inexplicable phenomena 'in and above the Earth's atmosphere'.[47] It was a topic that interested Koestler, as evidenced by the numerous newspaper cuttings on it to be found in his papers.[48] He later said he had enjoyed Steven Spielberg's *Close Encounters of the Third Kind* (1977).[49] He was also involved in the short-lived KIB Foundation to support para-psychology. In 1980 he also helped finance a centennial event for Jabotinsky, his Zionist mentor of the 1920s, although he was not well enough to attend himself.[50] Koestler remained an important establishment figure. The Hoover Institution at Stanford University wrote to him in 1978 to offer to house his personal archive, and he was the recipient of a telegram from the German president Karl

'Acute and moving', the portrait head of Koestler by Daphne Hardy Henrion.

Carstens on his 75th birthday in 1980.[51] In international political affairs, Koestler was angered and upset by the suppression of the Solidarity movement in Poland in 1981–2, the later success of which he did not live to witness.[52]

The last tantalizing aspect of Koestler's final years was the apparent gradual shift in his political views. Before she became prime minister, Margaret Thatcher visited Koestler, and presumably admired the anti-Communist stance of the middle part of his career.

It is extraordinary to think of this former Communist receiving a personal visit from the future 'Iron Lady', even if Koestler professed to be 'unexcited' by contemporary politics.[53] They had more in common than an antipathy towards Stalinism. Koestler was opposed to the policy of strikes and aggressive unionism, and despite having known many members of the Labour Party leadership personally, he voted for Thatcher in 1979. She won the election, but Koestler was too ill to accept her invitation to a Downing Street reception.[54]

7

A Reputation Ruined?

In a foreword to Suzanne Labin's *Stalin's Russia* (1949), Koestler wrote: 'The main difficulty about Russia is to get at the facts and to put them before the public.' He continued, 'The myth addict, impervious to argument, incredulous of the sincerity of any criticism, can only be cured by a shock-therapy of facts.'[1] Thus spoke someone who had experienced the front line of twentieth-century propaganda journalism both as propagandist and as the target of misinformation. Something similar could be said of biographers and the biomyths they create and question, as the main difficulty in biography is to get at the facts and to put them into a coherent order, while maintaining a sustained narrative. It is all too easy to lapse into myth.

Whether or not Koestler became less committed to rationalism (or simply more credulous) with age, he was someone who was intimately familiar with the machinations of reputation management and character assassination. His careful crafting of his life story could neither prevent its unravelling, nor the damage to his intellectual persona, in the aftermath of his death. There are even moments in his life and work – such as the apparent implicit autobiographical self-criticism of his novel *Arrival and Departure*, which contains a warning about biographical interpretations ('The clown and the lion are both there, interwoven in the same pattern'), or the decision not to continue his autobiographical project – where one wonders if Koestler had long anticipated the biographers' dispute that was eventually to come (*AD*, pp. 213–14). Certainly, the anthology of extracts from selected works that he published in 1980, titled *From Bricks to Babel*, was an attempt to secure his intellectual legacy, as well as to make particular claims about his life story. But the Koestlers' joint suicide, and the rape claim made against Arthur, would soon tarnish a literary reputation that was already wearing thin.

Around 1979 Koestler had been diagnosed with Parkinson's disease and was later also diagnosed with leukaemia. Having been a member of the Voluntary Euthanasia Society (VES) for over ten years, Koestler signed a living will in April 1980, asking not be kept alive by artificial means and allowing doctors to hasten his end with painkilling drugs if needs be.[2] He also wrote a preface for a pamphlet of the VES titled *A Guide to Self-deliverance*, published in 1981, in which he stated that euthanasia, like obstetrics, was 'the natural corrective to a biological handicap', and voiced his fears about a botched suicide attempt.[3] Since his first attempt in 1934, Koestler had contemplated suicide several times: his dialogue with death seems almost to have been lifelong.

Koestler wrote a suicide note in June 1982, but it was another eight months before he finally decided to go through with it. He was worried about Cynthia's future after his death, and confided in Celia, Mamaine's sister, who was a regular visitor of the Koestlers. Celia offered to take Cynthia in if needs be, although there was no mention of suicide.[4] When it came to it, Cynthia joined him. In the last week of February 1983, Cynthia cancelled outstanding appointments and left notes for the cleaner, doctor and lawyer. She also had their dog put down. Arthur and Cynthia committed suicide by taking Tuinal tablets with whisky and wine. Koestler had access to the right practical information, as *A Guide to Self-deliverance* contained information on how to commit suicide effectively. It was a popular publication at the time and membership of the society was boosted by the publicity surrounding the guide, leading to more than 6,000 new members. The booklet was later at the centre

Arthur and Cynthia Koestler committed suicide together in 1983.

of a legal dispute in April 1983, only weeks after the Koestlers' deaths. Although distributing the book was not deemed necessarily unlawful, the doubt cast on the booklet's legality was enough to stop the Voluntary Euthanasia Society from continuing to print it.[5]

Cynthia was only 55 years old at the time of her death and many would say her death was needless, that she was someone with much left to live for. She must have seen it otherwise. Most of her adult life had been lived in Koestler's shadow, although she had worked independently in London, Paris and New York. She had also briefly been married to an American editor, but the marriage lasted only months and was over by the summer of 1953. Cynthia never had children. She had been pregnant at least five times, and four times by Koestler, but had an abortion each time. For very many years she accepted a secondary status to other women in Koestler's life, at first during his relationship with Mamaine, and later with other lovers. Despite her ambiguous position in Koestler's life, she did not walk away, even when he tried to get rid of her. At some emotional level, their relationship must have functioned well, for her, as well as for him. Shortly before her death she was described as a 'gentle, soft, sad woman', with the 'slightly numb Buddhist detachment of one who has spent a lifetime in surrender of her will to another'.[6]

Outwardly, she may have frequently been a peripheral presence, but she was a part of Koestler's life for over thirty years. At least one observer noted her tenacity, perhaps derived from the aftermath of her father's drug addiction. An enthusiastic gardener, she shared non-academic interests with Arthur, such as his love of dogs, and was as capable as anyone of living up to his unreformed expectations of what a wife should be. When it came to it, she made a clear choice to commit suicide with him, reportedly dressing up in her best clothes every day for the week beforehand.[7] In light of this knowledge, the notion that Cynthia had no choice, which was discussed in the aftermath of the suicides, is difficult to accept.[8] It is also important to remember that, in as much as it is sometimes an important influence, both Arthur and Cynthia had a family history of suicide. It was a private and clearly personal decision. They left an unfinished joint autobiography behind, begun in 1982, and later published as *Stranger on the Square* (1984).

Manès Sperber was among those who found the news of the Koestler suicides very difficult to accept.[9] Apart from his personal moral antipathy towards suicide, one reason may have been his and Arthur's parallel paths, as Koestler's life had mirrored Sperber's in various ways. They were the same age; they both began publishing in Austrian newspapers at a very young age; became Communists; lived in Berlin; worked in Paris; travelled to the Soviet Union; and became disillusioned with Stalinist Communism. The difference was mostly that Sperber did these things first, but Koestler had broader interests and more material success.[10] Likewise Eva Hay, who had been present at Koestler's first marriage to Dorothee Ascher, regretted Koestler's decision to let Cynthia commit suicide with him.[11]

In the years before the Koestler suicides, the Voluntary Euthanasia Society (at that point also known as EXIT) was at the centre of the Reed-Lyons affair, another high-profile case about the legality of assisted suicide. Its secretary, Nicholas Reed, and a volunteer, Mark Lyons, were tried in 1981 for aiding and abetting suicide. Reed was jailed for two years, while Lyons was given a suspended sentence. The case did substantial damage to the society's reputation, as some of those who were helped to commit suicide may not have had the capacity to decide freely, since they had been suffering from mental illness or alcoholism.[12] Then, as now, opinion was split on the ethics of assisted dying and the Koestler suicides only added fuel to an existing fire.

In biographical terms, the scandal of the Koestler suicides has since been eclipsed by an even greater one, namely the accusation, made over a decade after his death, that Koestler had raped the filmmaker Jill Craigie in the 1950s. One of the disputes between his biographers is how to interpret the claim of so-called acquaintance rape made against Koestler. The allegations were revealed by one biographer and later confirmed but mitigated by another, while others have sought to defend Koestler. In understanding the narration of sexual violence, this process of mitigation is of the utmost interest, for it reveals how far-reaching sexual violence is as a biographical and cultural problem.

Although the claim was not made public until the 1990s, it referred to an event in 1952. At the time, Koestler was an internationally famous author at the height of his career. His marriage to Mamaine having broken down, Koestler had moved back to Britain from America and was house-hunting in London. He was friends with Michael Foot, then the Labour MP for Plymouth Davenport, who many years later would become the leader of the Labour Party. Koestler had hosted Foot and his wife at his house in France a year before. The alleged incident happened on 4 May 1952, when Koestler had rung Foot's home and, having found only his wife at home, asked her to show him round Hampstead.

Michael Foot's wife was Jill Craigie, a film director, and it was she who made the rape claim at a dinner party at her home in 1994 or 1995. She made the claim more than ten years after Koestler's death and to a group of well-connected personal friends, including the author Salman Rushdie and the journalist Jon Snow. Exactly what happened on the day in 1952 is not entirely clear (Koestler's diary entry is uninformative, and Craigie waited a very long time before telling her story) but the accounts by the Koestler biographer Michael Scammell and the Craigie biographer Carl Rollyson concur on the main points. In short, Koestler had invited himself over and had got drunk while looking around the neighbourhood with Craigie (although she remained sober). Koestler asked Craigie to make him lunch and then pressured her into having sex with him.

Craigie later said she had told a fellow film director, Ronald Neame, but according to Michael Scammell, when Neame was asked about it in 1998, 'he remembered the details differently and couldn't remember any mention of violence'.[13] Perhaps she felt unable to tell Neame the whole truth, and it seems that either she (or just possibly her husband) attempted to suppress the episode. She did not turn down a lunch invitation with Koestler and Foot at the House of Commons only weeks later. It is not necessary to know much about Britain in the 1950s to see this as a plausible scenario, or to empathize with the psychology of a woman who acted in this way.

The story was broken by David Cesarani in his 1998 biography of Koestler, *Arthur Koestler: The Homeless Mind*. He incorporates it quite matter-of-factly into a chapter about Koestler's return to London in 1952. He recounts how, according to Craigie, the encounter was violent, with Koestler pulling her hair and banging her head repeatedly against the floor. At first she was able to get away from him and considered going to the police, but then foolishly went back into the room. Cesarani writes that 'she was scared that [reporting Koestler to the police] would lead to awful

Jill Craigie with her husband, Labour Party leader Michael Foot, in 1983.

publicity for her and Michael. She would be accusing a world-famous novelist of rape; they had been on a pub crawl and she had admitted him into her home by herself. It did not look good.'[14]

Cesarani was convinced the allegation was true. Consequently, in the 'authorized' Koestler biography by Michael Scammell, which was published in 2009, the narrative of the Koestler-Craigie encounter became one of the most important aspects, not least as a form of reply to Cesarani. While Michael Scammell ultimately concedes Koestler's likely guilt, it should also be noted that in terms of rhetoric, he does a lot to suggest that Koestler might equally well be innocent. This can be attributed to the fact that, as Carl Rollyson documents using extracts from Scammell's correspondence with Michael Foot, Scammell had originally not believed Craigie's story but came to change his mind.[15] Rollyson, in his more recent *A Private Life of Michael Foot* (2015), is also certain Koestler raped Craigie, and even lists two other rapes Koestler is alleged to have committed. Rollyson has also speculated whether Foot may have known about his wife's rape all along, questioning whether Craigie would have talked about the incident in public if he had not.[16]

By contrast, Scammell concludes that 'the likeliest explanation is that behaviour that wasn't at the time seen as rape has since come to be regarded as such, and that it is necessary to keep both of the standards in mind when contemplating what happened' and laments that 'Craigie's story and Cesarani's embellishment of it have left a stain on Koestler's reputation far larger than he deserves and need to be kept in proportion.'[17] Yet the question of proportion can also be seen historically, as the penalty for rape under the Criminal Justice Act of 1948 was life imprisonment, but had previously been a sentence of penal servitude (that is, hard labour). Had Koestler been reported and convicted in 1952, however unlikely that might have been, he would have missed this fate by only four years.

Defenders of Koestler are usually concerned that the rape claim seems to negate his positive relationships and character traits. More importantly, there can be no recourse to retroactive justice. In Koestler's case, however, the biographer has little need of recourse to counterfactual history. His promiscuity and preference for aggressive sex has been well documented and therefore the characterization by Christian Buckard, a German biographer of Koestler, that the claim Koestler was a rapist was a 'vicious rumour' is implausible.[18] Similarly, when Tony Judt criticizes David Cesarani in his book *Reappraisals: Reflections on the Forgotten Twentieth Century* (2009) for being 'tedious and "sexually correct" about his account of Koestler's adventures', he makes the weak argument that because Cesarani is sententious and sensationalist about Koestler he is somehow ignorant of the supposed ambiguities surrounding sexual consent.[19]

Judt contended that if Koestler had been taken to court over the issue, he would have won. He also maintained that unless Koestler had been a racist, a financer of terrorism or a lifelong Communist, there was no reason why his sex life should have an impact on the interpretation of his work.[20] Koestler's former girlfriend and lifelong friend Daphne Hardy Henrion disputed the claims, saying that he was 'never violent' and that rape would have been 'out of character', while Joseph Strelka lamented the fact that the accusations led to the removal of Henrion's Koestler bust from display at the University of Edinburgh.[21] By contrast, Michael Scammell's position, albeit highly defensive, is broadly correct: it is simply impossible to exclude the possibility of Koestler having been guilty of sexual violence.

One reason why Koestler's defenders fail to convince is because they are seeking to stave off the inevitable reputational damage that accompanies the accusation of sexual violence. Rape claims impact upon the ability of the reader and writer of biography to empathize with the accused subject. More crucially, nothing is more hurtful to survivors and their families than to deny the possibility of it having happened. Craigie's great-nephew, John Foot, wrote to *The Observer* newspaper in 2010 to complain about a previous article dealing with the story in which he thought the topic was not taken seriously enough. He wrote 'My great-aunt was raped, violently, in her own home, by Koestler. She was not "raped", and Koestler was not a "sexual adventurer", but a rapist.'[22] Dealing with the lack of historical justice by placing the event in inverted commas is, as Foot rightly points out, unsatisfactory.

The fact that Cesarani's and Rollyson's interpretations have been disputed does not mean that they are false and Judt's points about interpretation do not ring true. Koestler's life does relate to his work. His writing contains a male–female rape scene (in *Thieves in the Night*) and a description of coercive sex (in the earlier *Arrival and Departure*). The story of Koestler's alleged rape of Craigie is uncanny, as it closely mirrors the disturbing scene in *Arrival and Departure*, which had been written around ten years before. There an emotionally vulnerable (and potentially bisexual) woman, Odette, is physically coerced into sex by the novel's main protagonist, Peter

Slavek, who, if not quite an auto-fictional self-representation of Koestler, has much in common as a character with his literary creator. What is remarkable is the degree of awareness Koestler shows about the need for consent, as the character Peter Slavek is shown to disregard it. Odette even tells Peter, 'if you knock a woman about for long enough and get on her nerves, there comes a moment when she suddenly feels how silly all this struggling and kicking is' (*AD*, p. 55). While Saul Bellow, writing in the *New York Times Book Review* in 1943, thought Koestler brave for not providing easy answers to common conflicts in private (or public) morality, today we read this passage differently.[23] Did Koestler, ever keen to write from experience, perhaps describe an event that really took place? Is it possible to read scenes like this in Koestler's fiction neutrally, or at least 'unbiographically', with the knowledge that he may have committed rape, even on multiple occasions?

It is widely assumed that the rape accusation has put people off reading Koestler, but even contemporary critics felt uneasy about his portrayals of sex. Writing about *Thieves in the Night*, V. S. Pritchett said 'rape or lust without love is a special interest of Koestler's.'[24] Put simply, if, in light of the above (fiction included), one was asked 'Was Koestler a rapist?', the answer would have to be 'very possibly.' The problem for his potential readership, especially given his reputation as an author of autobiography, is that when an (auto-) biographical subject has been charged with a crime as stigmatized as rape, the reader and writer no longer want to identify with the subject. They may wish to criticize or reject Koestler. Alternatively, they may attempt to reject claims that they find disturbing and deny their possibility. Regardless of which direction the reader chooses, they inevitably have to negotiate the problem of empathy. Instead of the more forgivable archetype of the reformed criminal, they are confronted with an image of Koestler as a disgraced hero.

It is not a topic that will now ever be dissociated from Koestler's life. Even beyond the treatment of sexual violence in his work, the controversy is all too easy to associate with other negative aspects of Koestler's personality. Writing in her memoirs only a few years before the scandal broke, Eva Hay described her dislike of hysterical, over-sensitive and aggressive types such as Koestler (although she and her husband were rarely at the receiving end). She claimed never to have felt relaxed or secure in Koestler's company.[25] In light of Koestler's reputation for sexual predation, as well as for having hissy fits, it is not difficult to understand why. But it is a damaged and insecure rather than malign individual who comes through in the portrayal of a loveless encounter with a fictionalized Koestler in Simone de Beauvoir's novel *The Mandarins*. David Cesarani thought it more perceptive than any of Koestler's accounts of himself, or even of others.[26]

Beauvoir gives Koestler a Russian alter ego, just as Koestler did in his novels. Victor Scriassine is an intense, direct man who carries the woes of the wartime world on his shoulders, and has recently returned to Paris from exile in America (at the point at which the novel begins, in late 1944 and early 1945, the real-life Koestler was en route from London to Tel Aviv). Scriassine pursues the psycho-analyst Anne over drinks at the Ritz. The 39-year-old Anne lets herself be provoked into saying yes to Scriassine's unromantic propositioning. She describes her confusion, her lack of attraction and her lies about how much she enjoyed it. She is afraid of seeming like a bourgeois prude. Anne even says that she does not regret her decision, as she was trying to prove something to herself. But Scriassine is portrayed as someone suffering from deep insecurities, a man who does not respect women as equals, and someone with a powerful need for emotional endorsement. Anne sums up her mistake pithily when she says, 'A man, I discovered, isn't a Turkish bath.'[27]

Today Koestler is no longer as well-known as he once was and the rape claim is certainly not the only reason for his diminishing fame. Scammell has suggested two factors: the 'bewildering variety' of

Koestler's work and his place outside national literary canons.[28] Koestler does not fit in easily to anyone's heritage. Similarly, Strelka attributes Koestler's 'homelessness' to the fact that he was the product of a society that was gradually eradicated, that of the former Austria-Hungary. Strelka sees Koestler as belonging to the special class of 'Old Austrians', a designation for those who are perceived as belonging to the country's cultural heritage, even if they lived and worked beyond its post-1918 borders. Yet it is fair to say that Austria has not claimed Koestler for its own, despite *Darkness at Noon* having been written in German. There is also the question of Koestler's literary merit. Harold Bloom, for example, has deemed *Darkness at Noon* a 'period piece', destined to 'last up to three generations' and then 'vanish forever'.[29]

It would be foolish to try to predict the future. What can be said is that the story of Koestler's life reveals his many shortcomings and prevents anyone from putting him on too high a pedestal. His shift from literature, journalism and autobiography to meta-biology certainly did not help Koestler's reputation; nor did the fact that Cynthia's decision to commit suicide with him left Koestler's legacy without an obvious guardian. The dispute over 'what' Koestler was, or what he stood for, persists. Depending on whose account you read, Koestler is a journalist, an anti-Communist, a typical cosmopolitan Jew, a Zionist, a literary author, a science writer, a maverick, or (dare one add) a rapist. These disputes around Koestler's biographical image mask the value of his ideas, his books, the things he fought for and the way he saw himself. It is unhelpful to try and place Koestler in boxes labelled 'Jewish', 'journalist' or 'destined for the scrapheap'. The two major tasks he set himself, to bear witness to the suffering caused by totalitarianism and to try to counteract the technological twentieth century's paradoxical disinterest in the history of science, remain relevant today, regardless of what conclusions are drawn about his strength of character.

There are two ways in which Koestler's reputation has endured, even aside from his work, or the scandals of rape and suicide. With both the Koestler Trust and through his will, he tried to create a legacy for himself. His interest in the paranormal dated back to childhood. Cynthia and Arthur had both been inspired by Paul Kammerer's collecting of coincidences and Koestler wanted the study of this area to be his intellectual legacy. After their deaths, the estate of Arthur and Cynthia Koestler was to be used to establish a Chair in Parapsychology. It was a typically controversial choice. Karl Popper was asked to help find a home for Koestler's parapsychology bequest, but he refused, saying he did not regard it as a science and that he was not convinced the creation of an academic chair in the subject was helpful: parapsychology was mostly just in need of new ideas.[30]

Despite Popper's scepticism, the bequest has been a success. In 1985 an American psychologist named Robert Morris became the first Koestler Professor of Parapsychology at the University of Edinburgh, a position he held until his death in 2004. Morris believed parapsychology to be 'the study of anomalous influence (or communication, as some prefer) between organism and environment'. It was, he said, 'an interdisciplinary problem area, not a belief system'.[31] During his time in Edinburgh, Morris super-vised over a hundred undergraduate projects and thirty postgraduate projects and also became president of the psychology section of the British Science Association. Although there is no longer a Koestler Professor, the name lives on via the Koestler Parapsychology Unit (KPU), which celebrated its thirtieth anniversary in 2015, including a popular series of workshops at the Edinburgh Fringe. Over the course of its three decades, the Unit has generated over three hundred publications. It now also offers an annual online course in the history, academic practice and implications of parapsych-ology led by Caroline Watt, an academic psychologist who has been involved with the KPU since its foundation. Watt's book

Parapsychology: A Beginner's Guide is due to be published in 2016.[32] In the words of her colleague Peter Lamont, 'Bob [Morris] had a grand vision of parapsychology, which was not just about the existence of psi: it was about the very idea of it. For 30 years, thanks to him, the KPU has explored why the idea matters.'[33]

Similarly, the Koestler Trust, which was founded on Koestler's initiative in 1962, remains the UK's leading charity for prison arts. It organizes competitions across various categories for those in custody. Successful entries are then exhibited in London and regionally and also sold. The charity also supports former offenders by involving them in the organization. It has adapted and grown in the last decade in particular. Now more than 8,000 artworks are assessed each year and more than 50,000 visitors now attend Koestler Trust exhibitions. One of the most common reactions by participants in Koestler Trust competitions is that the recognition given to their work boosts their self-confidence and self-esteem. In the words of a participant, 'It boosted my confidence, and showed me what I personally can do when I get down to the things. It showed me I had a little hidden talent, which I never knew I had.'[34] The Trust celebrated its fiftieth anniversary in 2012 with a fundraising dinner at the Waldorf Hotel, the place where Koestler and David Astor first thought up the Koestler Trust, complete with a cake decorated by the Turner Prize winner Grayson Perry. It featured the words 'I wish a little cheap immortality', the reason Koestler once gave for his interest in setting up the prison arts awards. A book was also created to mark the occasion.[35]

In light of Koestler's life story and especially the rape claim made against him, the organizations that bear Koestler's name have to come to terms with a difficult legacy. Hitherto the Koestler Trust has been pragmatic, saying, 'We are a charity which celebrates the best achievements of people who have made grave mistakes in life, and Arthur Koestler continues to be an appropriate figure-head for this work.'[36] In trying to understand how to evaluate his

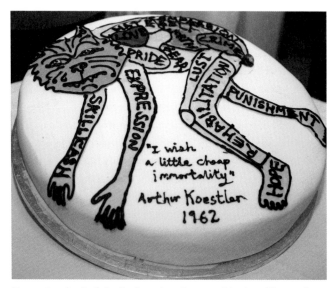

Grayson Perry's cake design for the 50th anniversary celebration of the Koestler Trust, 2012.

achievement, it may be helpful to think of him (as he once thought of himself) as a chronicler, an interdisciplinary diarist or documentarist. As such, he was a deeply flawed hero of his time, and his life can be both an inspiration and a warning for our own.

Maurice Cranston's claim for Koestler, repeated at a Royal Academy memorial event in 1983, that he was the twentieth-century writer whose reputation would last longest, was, even at the time, undoubtedly bold. That Koestler will be the one twentieth-century writer still being read in the year 2083 is of course unlikely. George Mikes suggested that Orwell was Koestler's 'rival and equal' in this regard.[37] Others, no doubt, would suggest other candidates, and with justification. Nevertheless, the comparison with Orwell is instructive, for his literary fame has endured while Koestler's has decreased – at least for now.

'With Koestler, as with Orwell, scepticism and research are crucial' – the words of Bernard Crick, speaking in Hawaii in 1987 on the writing of his Orwell biography.[38] This introductory life of Koestler may fall short on both. However, in writing this text, I do not want it to be either a hagiography or a debunking. Koestler's life was a fascinating one, however much it was a product of his own fantasy, and his work, always controversial, still has much to offer. At times Koestler doubted this, as many others have too. In one of the last interviews he gave, the interviewer reports Koestler's words as he surveys a bookcase filled with his own works and their many international translations. The insecurity in his voice is palpable: 'I must have had something to say. There must be something in it after all.'[39]

Chronology

1905   Birth of Arthur Koestler (also spelled: Kestler / Kősztler/ Köstler) on 5 September, the only child of Henrik and Adele Koestler, in Budapest, Austria-Hungary. Albert Einstein publishes his theory of special relativity.

1911   Attends progressive kindergarten run by Laura Striker, sister of Karl and Michael Polanyi.

1913   Bohr and Rutherford describe the structure of the atom.

1914   First World War begins. The family moves to Vienna.

1915   Arthur returns to Budapest to continue his schooling. Lives with his aunt and her family before his parents return.

1916   Death of Kaiser Franz Joseph I at Schloss Schönbrunn, Vienna. He is succeeded by his great-nephew, who becomes Kaiser Karl I.

1918   The First World War ends in defeat for Austria-Hungary. Kaiser Karl I withdraws from Vienna. Republic of German-Austria declared. The Aster Revolution in Hungary sees Count Mihály Karólyi made prime minister. Hungarian Democratic Republic declared in November.

1919   Dispute over Hungary's future borders leads to political Lives with chaos. Hungarian Republic of Councils, led by Communist Béla Kun, is declared in March. Romanian troops occupy Budapest in September. Admiral Horthy takes power. The Koestler family moves to Vienna. Arthur attends school in spa town of Baden, near Vienna.

1922   Koestler family moves to cheaper accommodation in Eisengasse in Vienna's 9th district. Arthur finishes school and begins studying engineering at the Higher School of Technology (now TU Wien). Joins Unitas, a Zionist fraternity.

1923   Arthur becomes president of Unitas and chair of all Zionist fraternities in Vienna.

1924   Meets leading Zionist Ze'ev (Vladimir) Jabotinsky. Arthur writes his first published article. Koestler family finances deteriorate.

1926   Koestler abandons his university studies and moves to Palestine to work on a kibbutz. Odd jobs in Haifa and Tel Aviv. First article in a major newspaper (*Neue Freie Presse*).

1927   Koestler works for the Ullstein newspapers in Berlin. Gains role as Middle East correspondent. Returns to Palestine. Georges Lemaître first suggests the Big Bang theory of the universe.

1929   Koestler requests a transfer and is given a job in Paris. Dissociates himself from Revisionist Zionists. Hubble publishes report confirming theory of the expanding universe.

1930   Works for Ullstein papers in Berlin. Becomes science editor. Interviews Einstein by telephone. First National Socialist landslide in Reichstag.

1931   Koestler reports from zeppelin voyage to the Arctic. Increasing politicization leads him to join Communist Party at the end of the year. Kurt Gödel's incompleteness theorems published.

1932   Koestler's Communist Party membership discovered by employers and he leaves his job. Member of Communist cell including Wilhelm

Reich. Leaves for year-long visit to the Soviet Union. Witnesses Ukrainian famine.

1933   Writes 'White Nights and Red Days'. Returns to Budapest for the summer. Moves to Paris to work for renowned propagandist Willi Münzenberg. He meets his future wife, Dorothee Ascher.

1934   Leaves Münzenberg job and co-writes *L'Encyclopédie de la vie sexuelle* (Paris, 1933) under a pseudonym for his entrepreneur cousin. Begins working on *The Gladiators*.

1935   Koestler and Ascher move to Zurich to live in Ascher's brother's apartment. They marry in June. For his cousin and to earn money, Koestler writes *Sexual Anomalies and Perversions* (London, 1936), based on the work of Magnus Hirschfeld. Koestler spends part of the summer in Budapest and visits Maria Klöpfer in Lugano. Koestler and Ascher return to Paris.

1936   Koestler continues work on *The Gladiators*. Koestler and Ascher spend summer with other writers on the Belgian coast. Outbreak of Spanish Civil War. Koestler travels via Lisbon to Seville to report from the Nationalist camp. He is recognized by a former Ullstein colleague and flees via Gibraltar. Writes *Menschenopfer Unerhört*. The show trials in Moscow begin. His childhood friend, Eva Striker, is arrested in Moscow.

1937   Koestler reports from Málaga. The city falls to Nationalist troops. Arrest and imprisonment in Seville. Writes *Spanish Testament* following release in May. Travels via Zurich to Belgrade to meet his parents, and from there to Greece and Palestine to report for the *News Chronicle*. *Spanish Testament* becomes his first best-seller. Eva Striker is released and deported. Reunion in London.

1938   Gives a speech in Paris critical of the Communist Party. Resigns his membership shortly afterwards. Finishes *The Gladiators*. The Sudetenland and Austria are annexed by Hitler's Germany.

1939   Edits the Parisian exile magazine *Die Zukunft*. Co-authors a third
        work on sexology for his cousin, published as *The Practice of Sex*
        (London, 1939). Spends summer in the South of France with Daphne
        Hardy. Begins work on *Darkness at Noon*. Britain and France declare
        war on Germany. Koestler is arrested in Paris and imprisoned at
        Le Vernet.

1940   Released from Le Vernet. Returns to Paris. Finishes *Darkness at Noon*
        (translated by Hardy), which is published later that year. Arrested
        again by French authorities. Escapes and joins the Foreign Legion
        under an assumed name. Germany invades France. Koestler deserts the
        army and escapes via Algeria and Morocco to Lisbon, and from there
        to the UK. Briefly imprisoned in London, released December 1940.

1941   Lives with Hardy in Kensington. Works on *Scum of the Earth*. Joins
        Pioneer Corps and moves to Ilfracombe, Devon. *Dialogue with Death*
        published. Pearl Harbor bombing. U.S. declares war on Germany.

1942   Transfers to Ministry of Information and discharged from army.
        Publishes the essay 'The Yogi and the Commissar'. Official
        American, British and Soviet acknowledgement of the Holocaust.

1943   Renewed involvement in Zionist politics. Soviet victory at Stalingrad.
        Arrival and Departure is published.

1944   Hungary occupied by Germany. Koestler begins relationship with
        Mamaine Paget. Normandy landings and liberation of Paris.

1945   Koestler in Palestine reporting for *The Times*. Begins work on *Thieves
        in the Night*. Liberation of Budapest. Fall of Berlin. Allied victories in
        Europe. Atom bombs dropped on Hiroshima and Nagasaki. End of
        Second World War. Koestler returns to England.

1946   Helps draft pamphlet of *A Palestine Munich?* with Richard Crossman
        and Michael Foot, advocating the creation of a Zionist state. *Thieves
        in the Night* is published. Koestler living in North Wales with
        Mamaine. His mother, Adele, arrives in the UK from Hungary.

Koestler and Mamaine visit Paris, meeting Sartre, Beauvoir and Camus. Koestler and Michael Polanyi meet in North Wales.

1947   United Nations Commission endorses the partition of Palestine. Partition of India and creation of Pakistan. Koestler begins work on *Insight and Outlook*. Becomes interested in extrasensory perception. Koestler and Mamaine revisit Paris.

1948   Koestler granted British citizenship. Tour of United States, followed by move to Israel following its creation in May. Arab–Israeli War. Koestler and Mamaine stay in Tel Aviv, later moving to Paris.

1949   Publication of *Insight and Outlook, Promise and Fulfilment* and *The God that Failed*. Cynthia Jefferies begins working for Koestler. Divorce from Dorothee Ascher. Koestler recruited by Congress for Cultural Freedom.

1950   Marriage to Mamaine in Paris. Major speech in Berlin. Buys house in Pennsylvania. McCarthyism begins.

1951   Mamaine and Koestler return to Europe. Cynthia is fired. Koestler meets Janine Detry de Marès. Koestler returns to Pennsylvania. *The Age of Longing* is published. Work on *Arrow in the Blue*.

1952   Relationship with Mamaine ends. Koestler buys house in London. *Arrow in the Blue* is published. Death of George VI.

1953   Work on *The Invisible Writing*. Divorce from Mamaine. Koestler has affairs with Janetta Jackson and Janine Detry de Marès. Buys home on Ischia with Detry de Marès. Coronation of Elizabeth II. Discovery of DNA by Watson, Crick and others.

1954   Mamaine's death in London. Sale of home in Pennsylvania. Detry de Marès announces pregnancy.

1955   Relationship with Elizabeth Jane Howard. Birth of supposed daughter with Detry de Marès. Howard has abortion and their

relationship ends. Begins work on *Reflections on Hanging*.
Cynthia re-employed as secretary. Koestler buys Long Barn.
Allied occupation of Austria and West Germany ends.

1956   Relationship with Cynthia. *Reflections on Hanging* is published.
The revolution in Hungary is suppressed by the Soviet Union.
Suez Crisis. Koestler maintains public silence on political topics.

1957   Work on *The Sleepwalkers*. Attends European Forum in Alpbach
for the first time. Koestler meets Eva Auer. Arranges for house to
be built in Alpbach. Relationship with Cynthia falters.

1959   Publication of *The Sleepwalkers*. C. P. Snow's 'Two Cultures' lecture.
Koestler sells Long Barn. Summers now spent regularly in Alpbach.

1960   Koestler visits India and Japan. Publishes *The Lotus and the Robot*.
His mother's death.

1961   Koestler visits USA. Experimentation with psilocybin.

1962   Work on *The Act of Creation*. Koestler Awards for prison arts
launched.

1964   *The Act of Creation* is published.

1965   Koestler marries Cynthia Jefferies in New York. Fellowship
at Stanford.

1967   Publication of *The Ghost in the Machine*. Six-day War between Israel
and neighbouring states.

1968   Prague Spring and wave of protests. Koestler awarded the Sonning
Prize. 'Beyond Reductionism' symposium in Alpbach. Trip to
Australia.

1969   Speaks at the Nobel Symposium in Stockholm. Joins Voluntary
Euthanasia Society. Abolition of hanging in the UK.

1970   Work on *The Case of the Midwife Toad*. Buys house in Suffolk.
       Cynthia learns truth about her father's death.

1971   *The Case of the Midwife Toad* is published. Inspired by Kammerer's
       example, Arthur and Cynthia collect accounts of coincidences.

1972   Awarded CBE. *The Call Girls* is published. *The Roots of Coincidence*
       is published.

1973   Iain Hamilton begins writing his biography of Koestler. Britain joins
       the European Economic Community.

1974   Koestler made a Companion of the Royal Society of Literature
       (C.Lit), its highest award.

1975   *Astride the Two Cultures*, a Festschrift for Koestler, is published.

1976   *The Thirteenth Tribe* is published.

1978   A summary of Koestler's works, *Janus. A Summing Up*, is published.

1979   Major strikes in the UK. Margaret Thatcher elected prime minister.
       Koestler is diagnosed with Parkinson's disease.

1980   *Bricks to Babel*, a collection of extracts from Koestler's books,
       introduced by the author, is published. Michael Foot becomes leader
       of the Labour Party.

1981   The suicide 'manual', *A Guide to Self-deliverance* is published, featuring
       an introduction by Koestler. Martial law is imposed in Poland.

1982   Koestler writes suicide note in June. Iain Hamilton's biography
       is published.

1983   Koestler commits suicide with Cynthia on 1 March.

References

Introduction: Why Koestler?

1 Maurice Cranston, Review of 'Iain Hamilton, *Koestler: A Biography*', *American Spectator* (March 1983), pp. 32–4 (p. 32).
2 Ibid., p. 34.
3 Tibor Fischer, Review of '*Koestler: The Indispensable Intellectual* by Michael Scammell', www.theguardian.com, 17 April 2010.
4 See for example David Cesarani, reply by Julian Barnes, 'Morality and Arthur Koestler', www.nybooks.com, 27 April 2000.

1 From Budapest to Palestine

1 Paul Ignotus, 'The Hungary of Michael Polanyi', in *The Logic of Personal Knowledge. Essays Presented to Michael Polanyi on his Seventieth Birthday* (London, 1961), pp. 3–12.
2 Pat Kirkham, 'Eva Zeisel: Design Legend, 1906–2011', in *Eva Zeisel: Life, Design, and Beauty*, ed. Pat Kirkham, Pat Moore and Pirco Wolfframm (San Francisco, CA, 2013), pp. 9–43 (pp. 14–18). See also William Taussig Scott and Martin X. Moleski, *Michael Polanyi: Scientist and Philosopher* (Oxford, 2005), p. 29.
3 Michael Scammell, *Koestler: The Literary and Political Odyssey of a Twentieth-century Skeptic* (New York, 2009), pp. 50–51.
4 Ibid., p. 7.
5 Duncan Fallowell, 'Arthur Koestler, The Art of Fiction No. 80' (1984), www.theparisreview.org, accessed 14 December 2015.

6 George Clare, *Last Waltz in Vienna: The Destruction of a Family, 1842–1942* (London, 1982), p. 85.

7 Christian Buckard, *Koestler. Ein extremes Leben 1905–1983* (Munich, 2004), p. 15.

8 John Lukacs, *Budapest 1900: A Historical Portrait of a City and its Culture* (New York, 1988), pp. 95–6.

9 Steven Beller, 'Introduction', in *Rethinking Vienna 1900*, ed. Steven Beller (New York and Oxford, 2001), pp. 1–25 (p. 18).

10 Buckard, *Koestler*, p. 15.

11 Iain Hamilton, *Koestler: A Biography* (London, 1982), p. 3.

12 Lisa Silverman, 'Reconsidering the Margins', *Journal of Modern Jewish Studies*, VIII/1 (2009), pp. 103–20 (p. 115).

13 Scammell, *Koestler*, pp. 16–17.

14 Richard Freadman, *Threads of a Life: Autobiography and the Will* (Chicago, IL, 2001), p. 177.

15 Scammell, *Koestler*, p. 22.

16 Ibid., pp. 23–6.

17 Ibid., pp. 15–16; p. 26.

18 On Herzl see Jacques Le Rider, *Modernity and Crises of Identity: Culture and Society in Fin-de-siècle Vienna*, trans. Rosemary Morris (Cambridge, 1993), p. 216.

19 Nick Reynold, *Britain's Unfulfilled Mandate for Palestine* (London, 2014), p. 41.

20 Scammell, *Koestler*, p. 39.

21 See Wiener Konzerthaus – Archivdatenbank (Vienna Konzerthaus – Archive Database), Events 7596 and 7568, konzerthaus.at, accessed 14 December 2015.

22 Katharina Prager, 'Karl Kraus Online'. Wienbibliothek im Rathaus / Ludwig Boltzmann Institut für Geschichte und Theorie der Biographie (2015), www.kraus.wienbibliothek.at, accessed 14 December 2015.

23 Scammell, *Koestler*, p. 42.

24 See historical city registration details for Arthur Köstler and Heinrich Köstler, City of Vienna, Magistratsabteilung 8.

25 Hamilton, *Koestler*, p. 9; David Cesarani, *Arthur Koestler: The Homeless Mind* (London, 1998), p. 44.

26 Ze'ev (Vladimir) Jabotinsky to Joanna Jabotinsky, 13 November 1925.

Jabotinsky Institute in Israel, 4613 (A1–2/35/5), en.jabotinsky.org, accessed 14 December 2015. Translation my own. See also Hillel Halkin, *Jabotinsky: A Life* (New Haven, CT, and London, 2014), pp. 158–9.

27 Cesarani, *Arthur Koestler*, p. 33.

2 Zionist and Communist

1 See John Oppenheimer, ed., *Lexikon des Judentums* (Gütersloh, Vienna etc., 1971), pp. 897–8.

2 National Library of Israel, 'Doar Hayom', *Historical Jewish Press*, web.nli.org.il/sites/JPress/English, accessed 14 December 2015.

3 Michael Scammell, *Koestler: The Literary and Political Odyssey of a Twentieth-century Skeptic* (New York, 2009), p. 65.

4 Nick Reynolds, *Britain's Unfulfilled Mandate for Palestine* (London, 2014), pp. 118–24. For figures see p. 123.

5 Mamaine Koestler, *Living with Koestler: Mamaine Koestler's Letters, 1945–51*, ed. Celia Goodman (New York, 1985), p. 114.

6 Pat Kirkham, 'Eva Zeisel: Design Legend, 1906–2011', in *Eva Zeisel: Life, Design, and Beauty*, ed. Pat Kirkham, Pat Moore and Pirco Wolfframm (San Francisco, CA, 2013), pp. 9–43 (pp. 21–4).

7 Ibid., p. 25.

8 Iain Hamilton, *Koestler: A Biography* (London, 1982), p. 42.

9 David Cesarani, *Arthur Koestler: The Homeless Mind* (London, 1998), p. 62.

10 Scammell, *Koestler*, pp. 78–9.

11 Christian Buckard, *Koestler. Ein extremes Leben 1905–1983* (Munich, 2004), p. 111.

12 Hamilton, *Koestler*, p. 17.

13 Scammell, *Koestler*, p. 74.

14 Ibid., pp. 85–6.

15 For a comparison see David Craig and Michael Egan, 'Can Literature be Evidence?', *Minnesota Review*, IV (1975), pp. 85–105 (pp. 91–3).

16 See Langston Hughes, *Collected Works*, vol. XIV: *Autobiography: I Wonder as I Wander*, ed. Joseph McLaren (Columbia, MO, 2003), pp. 133–59.

17 As collaborative, popular non-fiction works, the three books in the broad area of 'sexology' that Koestler wrote or co-wrote for

Aldor will not be discussed in detail here. See Scammell, *Koestler*, p. 107; p. 119; p. 170.

18 Hamilton, *Koestler*, pp. 29–30.

19 Koestler said that the wedding took place in March (*IW*, p. 279). Scammell gives the date as 22 June 1935 (*Koestler*, p. 118). János Szabó, following Andreas Saurer, gives the date of the Hay wedding as 6 June and that of the Koestler wedding as 19 June. See Janós Szabó, *Der 'vollkommene Macher' Julius Hay. Ein Dramatiker im Bann der Geschichte* (Munich, 1992), p. 34, n. 60.

20 Scammell, *Koestler*, p. 119.

21 See Andor Németh, 'Memories of Koestler (Excerpts from a Memoir)', *Hungarian Quarterly*, CLXXVII (2005), pp. 11–22 (pp. 17–18).

22 See Németh's account of Kloepfer, ibid., pp. 18–20.

23 See Murray A. Sperber, 'Looking Back on Koestler's Spanish War', in *Arthur Koestler: A Collection of Critical Essays*, ed. Murray Sperber (Englewood Cliffs, NJ, 1977), pp. 109–21.

24 Matthew Taunton, '2 +2 = 5: The Politics of Number in Writing about the Soviet Union', *Textual Practice*, XXIX/5 (2015), pp. 993–1016 (p. 1012).

25 Scammell, *Koestler*, pp. 142–4.

26 Joseph Strelka, *Arthur Koestler. Autor – Kämpfer – Visionär* (Tübingen, 2006), p. 43.

27 Louis Menand, 'Introduction', in Arthur Koestler, *Dialogue with Death*, trans. Trevor and Phyllis Blewitt (Chicago, IL, 2011), pp. v–xv (pp. viii–ix).

28 See William Taussig Scott and Martin X. Moleski, *Michael Polanyi: Scientist and Philosopher* (Oxford, 2005), p. 163.

29 Kirkham, 'Eva Zeisel', p. 28.

30 'Ravich-Terzin, Iakov Aleksandrovich', *Kniga pamiati* (Book of Memory), www.uznal.org/book_of_memory.php, accessed 14 December 2015; 'Ravich-Terzin, Iakov Aleksandrovich', *Martirolog rasstreliannykh v Moskve i Moskovskoi oblasti* [Martyrology of those executed in Moscow and Moscow Region], 18656, Sakharov Center, www.sakharov-center.ru, accessed 14 December 2015.

31 Kirkham, 'Eva Zeisel', pp. 28–30. Ravich-Terzin was arrested around the same time as Eva's release. See also Jean Richards and Brent C. Brolin, eds, *Eva Zeisel: A Soviet Prison Memoir* (New York, 2012).

32 Scammell, *Koestler*, pp. 158–9.

33 *IW*, pp. 388–9; Scammell, *Koestler*, p. 160.

3 Documentarist

1 Karl Popper, *The Open Society and its Enemies* (London and New York, 2011), p. 165; p. 189.

2 Michael Scammell, *Koestler: The Literary and Political Odyssey of a Twentieth-century Skeptic* (New York, 2009), p. 162.

3 On Koestler's self-censorship on the subject of Republican crimes in Spain see Lee Congdon, *Seeing Red: Hungarian Intellectuals in Exile and the Challenge of Communism* (DeKalb, IL, 2001), pp. 49–51.

4 On 'literary reportage' see chap. 4, 'The "Elasticity" of Literary Reportage', in John C. Hartsock, *Literary Journalism and the Aesthetics of Experience* (Amherst and Boston, MA, 2016), pp. 82–123. Hartsock discusses the work of Egon Erwin Kisch in particular.

5 V. S. Pritchett, 'Koestler: A Guilty Figure', in *Arthur Koestler: A Collection of Critical Essays*, ed. Murray Sperber (Englewood Cliffs, NJ, 1977), pp. 53–68 (p. 67).

6 Brent D. Shaw, 'Spartacus Before Marx', Version 2.2 (November 2005), *Princeton/Stanford Working Papers in the Humanities*, www.princeton. edu/~pswpc, accessed 14 December 2015, pp. 16–18.

7 George Orwell, 'Arthur Koestler', in *Arthur Koestler*, ed. Sperber, pp. 13–24 (p. 17).

8 Pritchett, 'Koestler', p. 57.

9 See Duncan L. Cooper, 'Dalton Trumbo vs. Stanley Kubrick: The Historical Meaning of Spartacus', in *Spartacus: Film and History*, ed. Martin M. Winkler (Malden and Oxford, 2007), pp. 56–64.

10 Janet Flanner, *Paris was Yesterday, 1925–1939*, ed. Irving Drutman (New York, 1972), p. 220.

11 Scammell, *Koestler*, pp. 172–5.

12 Christian Buckard, *Koestler. Ein extremes Leben 1905–1983* (Munich, 2004), p. 161.

13 Scammell, *Koestler*, p. 177.

14 Hannah Arendt, *The Origins of Totalitarianism* (New York, 1951), p. 417.

15 Scammell, *Koestler*, pp. 180–81.

16 Iain Hamilton, *Koestler: A Biography* (London, 1982), p. 88.

17 Report by Kassel University, 10 August 2015, www.uni-kassel.de, accessed 14 December 2015.

18 Scammell, *Koestler*, p. 185.

19 *IW*, p. 421; Scammell, *Koestler*, p. 190.

20 Scammell, *Koestler*, p. 187; pp. 191–2.

21 Ibid., p. 181.

22 Pat Kirkham, 'Eva Zeisel: Design Legend, 1906–2011', in *Eva Zeisel: Life, Design, and Beauty*, ed. Pat Kirkham, Pat Moore and Pirco Wolfframm (San Francisco, CA, 2013), pp. 9–43 (p. 34).

23 Hamilton, *Koestler*, p. 49; David Cesarani, *Arthur Koestler: The Homeless Mind* (London, 1998), p. 2.

24 Pritchett, 'Koestler: A Guilty Figure', pp. 60–61.

25 See Astrid Erll, 'Generation in Literary History: Three Constellations of Generationality, Genealogy, and Memory', *New Literary History*, XLV/3 (2014), pp. 385–409 (p. 390).

26 Malcolm Cowley, 'Koestler: The Disenchanted', in *Arthur Koestler*, ed. Sperber, pp. 25–9 (p. 28).

27 Tony Judt, *Reappraisals: Reflections on the Forgotten Twentieth Century* (London, 2009), p. 40.

28 See Anna Krylova, 'The Tenacious Liberal Subject in Soviet Studies', *Kritika: Explorations in Russian and Eurasian History*, I/1 (2000), pp. 119–46 (pp. 124–6; 142–6).

29 Roger Berkowitz, 'Approaching Infinity: Dignity in Arthur Koestler's *Darkness at Noon*', *Philosophy and Literature*, XXXIII/2 (2009), pp. 296–314 (p. 300; p. 311).

30 Scammell, *Koestler*, p. 196; Koestler thought the title came from Milton (*IW*, p. 402).

31 Scammell, *Koestler*, p. 214.

32 Ibid., p. 202.

33 Ibid., pp. 208–9.

34 Ibid., p. 218. See also 'Lift Your Head, Comrade' (1942), Imperial War Museum, London, www.iwm.org.uk, accessed 14 December 2015.

35 Scammell, *Koestler*, pp. 211–13.

36 Ibid., pp. 229–31.

37 Orwell, 'Arthur Koestler', pp. 21–4.

38 Pritchett, 'Koestler: A Guilty Figure', p. 63.

39 'United Nations Declaration', Parliamentary Hansard (Commons), 17 December 1942.

40 Scammell, *Koestler*, pp. 229–30.

41 Ibid., pp. 231–7.

42 Ibid., p. 217.

43 Michael Fleming, *Auschwitz, the Allies and Censorship of the Holocaust* (Cambridge, 2014), p. 130; p. 239; p. 246.

44 Scammell, *Koestler*, p. 242.

45 Ibid., p. 264.

46 Ibid., p. 241; pp. 250–51.

47 Ibid., pp. 252–6.

48 Ibid., pp. 269–70.

49 *YC*, p. 18. The full original version is: 'L'homme n'est ni ange ni bête, et le malheur veut que qui veut faire l'ange fait la bête.' Blaise Pascal, *Pensées* (Paris, 1964), p. 164.

4 Infamy and Autobiography

1 See Elizabeth Jane Howard, *Slipstream: A Memoir* (London, 2003), p. 265; George Mikes, *Arthur Koestler: The Story of a Friendship* (London, 1983), p. 21.

2 Stephen Brockmann, *German Literary Culture at the Zero Hour* (London, 2004), pp. 158–9.

3 Richard Crossman and Michael Foot, *A Palestine Munich?* (London, 1946), p. 8; p. 31.

4 Koestler, 'Letter to a Parent of a British Soldier in Palestine', www.newstatesman.com, 16 August 1947. Republished online 15 January 2007.

5 Edmund Wilson, 'Arthur Koestler in Palestine', in *Arthur Koestler: A Collection of Critical Essays*, ed. Murray Sperber (Englewood Cliffs, NJ, 1977), pp. 44–7 (pp. 46–7).

6 Isaac Rosenfeld, 'Palestinian Ice Age', in *Arthur Koestler*, ed. Sperber, pp. 48–52 (p. 49).

7 Sharon Rotbard, 'Wall and Tower: The Mold of Israeli *adrikhalut*', in *City of Collision*, ed. Philipp Miselwitz and Tim Rieniets (Basel, Boston, and Berlin, 2006), pp. 102–12 (p. 106; p. 109).

8 The articles in questions were published under the title 'From a Special Correspondent Lately in Palestine' on 25–6 September 1945. See also Scammell, *Koestler*, p. 275; *IW*, p. 381.

9   Edward Said, *The Question of Palestine* (London and Henley, 1980),
    pp. 20–21.
10 Ibid.
11 Said, *Palestine*, p. 8; *TN*, pp. 150–52.
12 Said, *Palestine*, p. 38.
13 Martine Poulain, 'A Cold War Best-seller: The Reaction to Arthur
    Koestler's *Darkness at Noon* in France from 1945 to 1950', *Libraries &
    Culture*, XXXVI/1 (2001), pp. 172–84 (p. 174; p. 179). See also n. 25 and
    n. 27 (p. 182).
14 Ibid., p. 178.
15 Maurice Merleau-Ponty, 'Koestler's Dilemmas', in *Arthur Koestler*,
    ed. Sperber, pp. 69–85.
16 Michael Scammell, *Koestler: The Literary and Political Odyssey of a
    Twentieth-century Skeptic* (New York, 2009), p. 272.
17 Ibid., pp. 289–92.
18 Mamaine Koestler, *Living with Koestler: Mamaine Koestler's Letters
    1945–51*, ed. Celia Goodman (New York, 1985), p. 40.
19 Scammell, *Koestler*, pp. 292–303.
20 David Cesarani, *Arthur Koestler. The Homeless Mind* (London, 1998),
    p. 279; Scammell, *Koestler*, p. 303.
21 William Taussig Scott and Martin X. Moleski, *Michael Polanyi: Scientist
    and Philosopher* (Oxford, 2005), p. 200.
22 Cesarani, *Koestler*, p. 558.
23 Taussig Scott and Moleski, *Michael Polanyi*, p. 257; p. 276.
24 Iain Hamilton, *Koestler: A Biography* (London, 1982), p. 285.
25 Arthur Koestler, *Insight and Outlook: An Inquiry into the Common
    Foundations of Science, Art and Social Ethics* (London, 1949), pp. 371–80;
    see also *AC*, pp. 358–65.
26 James Duban, '"Oceanic Wonder": Arthur Koestler and Melville's
    Castaway', *Philosophy and Literature*, XXXII/2 (2011), pp. 371–4.
27 Mamaine Koestler, *Living with Koestler*, pp. 51–2.
28 Ibid., p. 59.
29 Scammell, *Koestler*, pp. 305–9.
30 Pat Kirkham, 'Eva Zeisel: Design Legend, 1906–2011', in *Eva Zeisel: Life,
    Design, and Beauty*, ed. Pat Kirkham, Pat Moore and Pirco Wolfframm
    (San Francisco, CA, 2013), pp. 9–43 (pp. 34–5).
31 Mamaine Koestler, *Living with Koestler*, pp. 67–9.

32 *Nakba* is the Arabic word for 'disaster'.

33 Scammell, *Koestler*, p. 329.

34 Mamaine Koestler, *Living with Koestler*, pp. 86–7.

35 Ibid., p. 86; pp. 93–4.

36 See Leslie Stein, *The Making of Modern Israel, 1948–1967* (Cambridge, 2009), pp. 37–8.

37 Scammell, *Koestler*, p. 331.

38 Mamaine Koestler, *Living with Koestler*, p. 88.

39 Scammell, *Koestler*, pp. 333–4.

40 Ibid., pp. 342–3.

41 Koestler, untitled essay, in *The God that Failed: Six Studies in Communism*, ed. Richard Crossman (London, 1950), pp. 25–82 (pp. 26–9).

42 Ibid., pp. 81–2.

43 Mamaine Koestler, *Living with Koestler*, p. 100.

44 Ibid., p. 120.

45 Scammell, *Koestler*, pp. 368–9.

46 Frances Stonor Saunders, *Who Paid the Piper? The CIA and the Cultural Cold War* (London, 2000), pp. 89–90.

47 Scammell, *Koestler*, pp. 348–9.

48 Ibid., pp. 376–8.

49 Mamaine Koestler, *Living with Koestler*, pp. 159–60.

50 Howard, *Slipstream*, p. 267.

51 Scammell, *Koestler*, p. 378.

52 Ibid., p. 381.

53 Ibid., p. 388.

54 Ibid., p. 392.

55 Mamaine Koestler, *Living with Koestler*, p. 179.

56 Ibid., p. 131; Scammell, *Koestler*, pp. 396–8.

57 Richard Freadman, *Threads of a Life: Autobiography and the Will* (Chicago, IL, 2001), p. 179.

58 Ibid., p. 176.

59 Scammell, *Koestler*, p. 411.

60 Stephen Spender, 'In Search of Penitence', in *Arthur Koestler*, ed. Sperber, pp. 100–108 (p. 103).

61 Scammell, *Koestler*, p. 423.

62 Mamaine Koestler, *Living with Koestler*, p. 116, pp. 135–6.

63 Ibid., p. 112.
64 Ibid., p. 114.
65 Ibid., p. 194.
66 Scammell, *Koestler*, pp. 423–4.
67 Ibid., p. 432.
68 Ibid., p. 442.
69 Ibid., p. 434; p. 532.
70 Howard, *Slipstream*, p. 269.
71 Scammell, *Koestler*, p. 438.
72 Arthur Koestler and Cynthia Koestler, *Stranger on the Square*
    (London, 1984), p. 219.
73 Koestler (writing as 'Vigil'), *Patterns of Murder: A Five Year Survey
    of Men and Women Executed in England, Scotland and Wales (1949–53)
    by Vigil of 'The Observer'* (London, 1956), p. 8.
74 Scammell, *Koestler*, p. 447.
75 Freadman describes Koestler's position on free will as having 'too many
    contradictions', *Threads of Life*, p. 203.
76 Mamaine Koestler, *Living with Koestler*, p. 186.
77 Matthew Taunton, '2 +2 = 5: The Politics of Number in Writing
    about the Soviet Union', *Textual Practice*, xxix/5 (2015), pp. 993–1016
    (pp. 1011–12); Freadman, *Threads of Life*, p. 199.

5 Science and Progress

1   Stephen Toulmin, 'The Book of Arthur', in *Arthur Koestler: A Collection
    of Critical Essays*, ed. Murray Sperber (Englewood Cliffs, NJ, 1977),
    pp. 167–79 (p. 168).
2   Arthur Koestler, *Bricks to Babel* (New York, 1980), p. 10; p. 321.
3   John Atkins, *Arthur Koestler* (London, 1956), p. 7, p. 42.
4   Michael Scammell, *Koestler: The Literary and Political Odyssey
    of a Twentieth-century Skeptic* (New York, 2009), p. 570.
5   Ibid., pp. 448–9.
6   Ibid., pp. 451–2.
7   Mary Jo Nye, *Michael Polanyi and His Generation: Origins of the Social
    Construction of Science* (Chicago, IL, 2011), p. 303.
8   Scammell, *Koestler*, p. 471.

9 Christian Buckard, *Koestler. Ein extremes Leben 1905–1983* (Munich, 2004), p. 307.

10 David Cesarani, *Arthur Koestler: The Homeless Mind* (London, 1998), p. 471.

11 Pál Ignotus and Arthur Koestler, '"The Contact Has Always Remained" – A Conversation Between Arthur Koestler and Pál Ignotus', *Hungarian Quarterly*, CLXXVII (2005), pp. 23–5 (p. 25).

12 Joseph Strelka, *Arthur Koestler. Autor – Kämpfer – Visionär* (Tübingen, 2006), p. 11.

13 Ibid., p. 8.

14 Scammell, *Koestler*, pp. 472–4.

15 Arthur Koestler to Karl Popper, undated, Karl Popper Library, Sig. 315.36, Hoover Institution Archive at Stanford University, California/ University of Klagenfurt Library.

16 Koestler Archive, University of Edinburgh, Arthur Koestler to Ludwig von Bertalanffy, 31 January 1966.

17 Scammell, *Koestler*, p. 462.

18 E. P. Snow, *The Two Cultures and a Second Look* (Cambridge, 1964), p. 81.

19 Thomas S. Kuhn, *The Structure of Scientific Revolutions*, 4th edn (Chicago, IL, and London, 2012).

20 *The Sleepwalkers* was republished by Penguin Classics in 2014.

21 Scammell, *Koestler*, p. 463.

22 Ibid., p. 476.

23 Ibid., p. 8.

24 Ibid., p. 16; p. 26.

25 Mamaine Koestler, *Living with Koestler: Mamaine Koestler's Letters, 1945–51*, ed. Celia Goodman (New York, 1985), p. 34.

26 Ibid., p. 149.

27 Scammell, *Koestler*, pp. 410–11.

28 Ibid., p. 417.

29 Ibid., p. 476.

30 Ibid., pp. 478–82.

31 Ibid., p. 474; pp. 492–3.

32 Sahotra Sarkar, 'Models of Reduction and Categories of Reductionism', *Synthese*, XCI (1992), pp. 167–94 (pp. 170–71).

33 See Robert J. Richards, *The Romantic Conception of Life: Science and Philosophy in the Age of Goethe* (Chicago, IL, and London, 2002), p. 2.

34 Scammell, *Koestler*, p. 477.

35 Ibid., pp. 485–6.

36 Ibid., p. 495.

37 Iain Hamilton, *Koestler: A Biography* (London, 1982), p. 331.

38 Scammell, *Koestler*, pp. 491–2.

39 Richard Freadman, *Threads of a Life: Autobiography and the Will* (Chicago, IL, 2001), p. 190.

40 *AC*, p. 246; Karl Popper, *The Logic of Scientific Discovery* (London and New York, 2002), p. 280.

41 James Duban, '"That Butcher, Imagination": Arthur Koestler and the Bisociated Narration of Philip Roth's *Indignation*', *Philip Roth Studies*, VIII/2 (2012), pp. 145–60 (p. 159).

42 See also James Duban, 'To Dazzle as Macbeth: Bisociated Drama in Philip Roth's *The Humbling*', *Comparative Drama*, XLVI/1 (2012), pp. 1–16; 'Arthur Koestler and Meyer Levin: The Trivial, the Tragic, and Rationalization Post Factum in Roth's "Eli, the Fanatic"', *Philip Roth Studies*, VII/2 (2011), pp. 171–86.

43 William Taussig Scott and Martin X. Moleski, *Michael Polanyi: Scientist and Philosopher* (Oxford, 2005), p. 258.

44 Michael Polanyi, 'The Creative Imagination', in *Toward a Unity of Knowledge*, ed. Marjorie Grene, *Psychological Issues*, VI/2 (1969), pp. 53–91 (p. 90).

45 Manfred Drack and Wilfried Apfalter, 'Is Paul A. Weiss' and Ludwig von Bertalanffy's System Thinking Still Valid Today?', *Systems Research and Behavioral Science*, XXIV (2007), pp. 537–46 (p. 542).

6 Uncertain Evolution

1 Henry Aiken, 'The Metaphysics of Arthur Koestler', in *Arthur Koestler: A Collection of Critical Essays*, ed. Murray Sperber (Englewood Cliffs, NJ, 1977), pp. 167–79 (p. 161).

2 A. J. Ayer, 'Koestlerkampf', www.lrb.co.uk, 20 May 1982, accessed 14 December 2015.

3 Michael Scammell, *Koestler: The Literary and Political Odyssey of a Twentieth-century Skeptic* (New York, 2009), pp. 502–5.

4 Iain Hamilton, *Koestler: A Biography* (London, 1982), p. 332.

5 Elizabeth Powers, 'The Sublime, "Über den Granit", and the Prehistory of Goethe's Science', *Goethe Yearbook*, xv (2008), pp. 35–56 (p. 47).

6 Michael Scammell, 'Decoding Koestler', in *Arthur Koestler: Ein heller Geist in dunkler Zeit*, ed. Robert G. Weigel (Tübingen, 2009), pp. 22–34 (p. 33).

7 Quoted in William Taussig Scott and Martin X. Moleski, *Michael Polanyi: Scientist and Philosopher* (Oxford, 2005), p. 265.

8 Scammell, *Koestler*, pp. 506–8.

9 Hamilton, *Koestler*, p. 354.

10 Agatha Christie, *Passenger to Frankfurt* (London, 2003), pp. 312–21.

11 Scammell, *Koestler*, pp. 512–15.

12 Stephen Toulmin, 'The Book of Arthur', in *Arthur Koestler*, ed. Sperber, pp. 167–79 (p. 175; p. 179).

13 Scammell, *Koestler*, pp. 508–10.

14 Joseph Strelka, *Arthur Koestler. Autor – Kämpfer – Visionär* (Tübingen, 2006), p. 126.

15 Scammell, *Koestler*, pp. 518–19.

16 Koestler, 'Rebellion in a Vacuum', in *The Place of Value in a World of Facts: Proceedings of the Nobel Symposium Stockholm, September 15–20 1969*, ed. Arne Tiselius and Sam Nillson (Stockholm, 1970), pp. 221–8 (p. 225: p. 228).

17 Koestler, 'The Urge to Self-destruction', in *The Place of Value*, ed. Tiselius and Nillson, pp. 297–305 (p. 301).

18 Voluntary Euthanasia Bill, Parliamentary Hansard, 25 March 1969, Lords Sitting.

19 Scammell, *Koestler*, p. 523. On 'displaced autobiography' see Max Saunders, 'Life-writing, Cultural Memory, and Literary Studies', in *Cultural Memory Studies: An International and Interdisciplinary Handbook*, ed. Astrid Erll and Ansgar Nünning (Berlin and New York, 2008), pp. 321–31 (p. 321).

20 Carl Brinitzer, *Heinrich Heine* (Hamburg, 1960); Hilde Spiel, *Fanny von Arnstein oder die Emanzipation* (Frankfurt, 1962); Robert Lucas, *Frieda von Richthofen. Ihr Leben mit D. H. Lawrence* (Munich, 1972).

21 Brian Howard Harrison, *Seeking a Role: The United Kingdom, 1951–1970* (Oxford, 2011), pp. 291–3.

22 Scammell, *Koestler*, p. 533.

23 Ibid., p. 534.

24 George Mikes, *Arthur Koestler: The Story of a Friendship* (London, 1983), p. 58.

25 See John Rodden, 'Personal Behavior, Biographical History, and Literary Reputation: The Case of George Orwell', *Biography*, XII/3 (1989), pp. 189–207 (pp. 195–6).

26 Scammell, *Koestler*, p. 537. Koestler Archive, University of Edinburgh, Koestler to J. B. Rhine, 5 August 1974 and 9 September 1974. See also Geller to Koestler, 14 August 1974; 21 August 1974. Hasted to Koestler, 22 August 1974. MS 2408/3.

27 Neil Ascherson, 'Raging Towards Utopia' [Review of *Koestler: The Indispensable Intellectual* by Michael Scammell], *London Review of Books*, www.lrb.co.uk, 22 April 2010.

28 Brigid Brophy, 'A Classic Non-contribution to Knowledge', *The Listener*, 3 January 1974, p. 22.

29 Mikes, *Arthur Koestler*, p. 71.

30 Scammell, *Koestler*, pp. 540–43.

31 Lee Congdon, 'Koestler's Hungarian Identity', www.c3.hu/~prophil (no. 3, 2005), accessed 14 December 2015.

32 Scammell, *Koestler*, p. 531; pp. 544–50.

33 Quoted in Hamilton, *Koestler*, p. 363.

34 Christian Buckard, *Koestler. Ein extremes Leben 1905–1983* (Munich, 2004), p. 336.

35 See Dmitrii Vasil'ev, 'Gorod i oblast' Saksin v svete novykh dannykh arkheologii' (The City and Region of Saksin in the Light of New Archaeological Data'), *Povolzhskaia arkheologiia*, II/12 (2015), pp. 189–267; Dmitrii Vasil'ev, ed., *Samosdel'skoe gorodishshe: voprosy izucheniia i interpretatsii. Sbornik nauchnykh statei* (The Samosdel'skoe Settlement: Questions of Study and Interpretation. A Collection of Academic Essays) (Astrakhan, 2011).

36 Buckard, *Koestler*, p. 18.

37 David Cesarani, *Arthur Koestler: The Homeless Mind* (London, 1998), p. 25.

38 Derek J. Penslar, 'Shlomo Sand's *The Invention of the Jewish People* and the End of the New History', *Israel Studies*, XVII/2 (2012), pp. 156–68 (pp. 157–8; p. 167).

39 Strelka, *Arthur Koestler*, p. 149.

40 See also Noa Sophie Kohler, 'Genes as a Historical Archive: On the Applicability of Genetic Research to Sociohistorical Questions:

The Debate on the Origins of Ashkenazi Jewry Revisited',
Perspectives in Biology and Medicine, LVII/1 (2014), pp. 105–17
(p. 110; p. 114).

41 Koestler Archive, MS 2411/3; MS 2439/3.

42 A. Costler and A. Willy, *Encyclopaedia of Sexual Knowledge*, ed. Norman Haire (New York, 1940), pp. 438–51.

43 Cesarani, *Koestler*, p. 66.

44 David Buckman, 'Daphne Hardy Henrion', www.independent.co.uk, first published 2003, republished online 21 October 2013.

45 Scammell, *Koestler*, p. 553.

46 Ibid., pp. 551–3.

47 Koestler Archive, MS 2350/1/47–48.

48 Ibid., MS 2408/1.

49 Duncan Fallowell, 'Arthur Koestler, The Art of Fiction No. 80' (1984), www.theparisreview.org, accessed 14 December 2015.

50 Buckard, *Koestler*, p. 344.

51 Koestler Archive, MS 2439/3; 2392/4.

52 Mikes, *Arthur Koestler*, p. 59.

53 Fallowell, 'Arthur Koestler, The Art of Fiction'.

54 Scammell, *Koestler*, p. 556; pp. 566–7.

7 A Reputation Ruined?

1 Arthur Koestler, 'Foreword', in Suzanne Labin, *Stalin's Russia*, trans. Edward Fitzgerald (London, 1950), pp. 7–10 (pp. 8–9).

2 Koestler Archive, Living Will, MS 2409/1.

3 Koestler Archive, Preface to *Guide to Self-deliverance*, MS 2409/3.

4 Michael Scammell, *Koestler: The Literary and Political Odyssey of a Twentieth-century Skeptic* (New York, 2009), pp. 561–2.

5 Margaret Otlowski, *Voluntary Euthanasia and the Common Law* (Oxford, 1997), pp. 270–71.

6 Duncan Fallowell, 'Arthur Koestler, The Art of Fiction No. 80' (1984), www.theparisreview.org, accessed 14 December 2015.

7 Scammell, *Koestler*, pp. 569–70.

8 Cf. David Cesarani, *Arthur Koestler: The Homeless Mind* (London, 1998), p. 552.

9   According to Leonhard Reinisch. See Reinisch, 'Gespräche mit Manès Sperber. Erinnerungen an eine dreißigjährige Freundschaft', in *Manès Sperber. Die Beiträge des Internationalen Symposiums gehalten anläßlich der Verleihung des Manès Sperber-Preises 1987*, ed. Victoria Lunzer-Talos (Vienna, 1987), pp. 6–21 (p. 15). There is no written evidence of this claim in the Reinisch-Sperber correspondence from 1983 (see Reinisch: Letter to Manès Sperber, 23 March 1983 and Sperber: Letter to Leonard Reinisch, 2 April 1983, Literaturarchiv der Österreichischen National-bibliothek, Sammlung Manès Sperber, Sign.: 2/B 996/12; 2B 1964/24).

10 See Rudolf Isler, 'Zwei Leben ein Jahrhundert. Manès Sperber und Arthur Koestler', in *Arthur Koestler: Ein heller Geist*, ed. Weigel, pp. 35–43 (pp. 35–6).

11 Eva Hay, *Auf beiden Seiten der Barrikade* (Leipzig, 1994), p. 313.

12 Otlowski, *Voluntary Euthanasia*, p. 271.

13 Scammell, *Koestler*, p. 407.

14 Cesarani, *Koestler*, p. 400.

15 Carl Rollyson, *To Be a Woman: The Life of Jill Craigie* (London, 2005), pp. 339–41.

16 Carl Rollyson, *A Private Life of Michael Foot* (Plymouth, 2015), pp. 20–21; pp. 296–7.

17 Scammell, *Koestler*, p. 408.

18 Christian Buckard, *Koestler. Ein extremes Leben 1905–1983* (Munich, 2004), p. 40.

19 Tony Judt, *Reappraisals: Reflections on the Forgotten Twentieth Century* (London, 2009), pp. 32–3.

20 Ibid., pp. 32–5.

21 'Daphne Hardy Henrion' (Obituary), www.telegraph.co.uk, 26 November 2003; Joseph Strelka, *Arthur Koestler. Autor – Kämpfer – Visionär* (Tübingen, 2006), p. 169. See also 'Women Force Removal of Koestler Bust', news.bbc.co.uk, 29 December 1998.

22 John Foot, 'Don't Defend Koestler's Deeds', *The Observer*, Letters, 28 February 2010. Foot was responding to Robert McCrum 'The Double Life of Arthur Koestler, Intellectual and Sexual Adventurer', www.theguardian.com, 21 February 2010.

23 Saul Bellow, 'A Revolutionist's Testament', in *Arthur Koestler: A Collection of Critical Essays*, ed. Murray Sperber (Englewood Cliffs, NJ, 1977), pp. 30–33 (p. 30).

24 V. S. Pritchett, 'Koestler: A Guilty Figure', in *Arthur Koestler*, ed. Sperber, pp. 53–68 (p. 66).

25 Hay, *Auf beiden Seiten*, p. 313.

26 Cesarani, *Koestler*, pp. 278–9.

27 Simone de Beauvoir, *The Mandarins*, trans. Leonard M. Friedman (London, 1957), pp. 88–101.

28 Michael Scammell, 'Decoding Koestler', in *Arthur Koestler: Ein heller Geist in dunkler Zeit*, ed. Robert G. Weigel (Tübingen, 2009), pp. 22–34 (pp. 23–5).

29 Harold Bloom, 'Introduction', in *Arthur Koestler's 'Darkness at Noon'*, ed. Bloom (Broomall, PA, 2004), pp. 1–2 (p. 1).

30 Karl Popper Library (Stanford/Klagenfurt), Karl Popper to Brian Inglis, 6 April 1983, Sig. 387.23.

31 Robert Morris, 'What I Shall Do with the Koestler Chair', *New Scientist*, 5 September 1985, p. 59.

32 For more information see koestlerunit.wordpress.com/blog and koestlerunit.wordpress.com/research-overview/archive-of-kpu-publications-by-author, accessed 14 December 2015.

33 Quoted in 'What do Bob Morris and the KPU mean to you?' (Koestler Unit video presentation), www.youtube.com, 23 July 2015.

34 The Koestler Trust, 'A Report on the 2013 Survey of Koestler Award Entrants. Report by Andrew Billington Associates. Based on a Survey Conducted by the Koestler Trust' (August 2014).

35 The Koestler Trust, *1962–2012: Celebrating 50 Years of Arts by Offenders* (London, 2012).

36 The Koestler Trust, 'Arthur Koestler, 1905–1983', www.koestlertrust. org.uk/pages/arthurkoestler.html, accessed 14 December 2015.

37 See George Mikes, *Arthur Koestler: The Story of a Friendship* (London, 1983), p. 59.

38 Bernard Crick, 'Orwell and Biography', *Biography*, X/4 (1987), pp. 283–300 (p. 293).

39 Fallowell, 'Arthur Koestler, The Art of Fiction'.

Select Bibliography

Books by Koestler

Von weißen Nächten und roten Tagen (Of White Nights and Red Days) [1933]
    (Vienna, 2013)
Die Erlebnisse des Genossen Piepvogel in der Emigration (Comrade
    Dicky-bird's Experiences in Exile) [1934] (Zurich, 2012)
Menschenopfer Unerhört (Untold Victims) (Paris, 1937)
Spanish Testament (London, 1937)
The Gladiators (London, 1939)
Darkness at Noon [1940] (New York, 1941)
Scum of the Earth (London, 1941)
Dialogue with Death [1942] (Chicago, IL, 2011)
Arrival and Departure (London, 1943)
The Yogi and the Commissar: And Other Essays [1945] (London, 1983)
Thieves in the Night [1946] (London, 1949)
Promise and Fulfilment: Palestine, 1917–1949 (London, 1949)
Insight and Outlook (London, 1949)
The Age of Longing (London, 1951)
Arrow in the Blue: An Autobiography (London, 1952)
The Invisible Writing: Autobiography, 1931–53 (London, 1954)
The Trail of the Dinosaur and Other Essays (London, 1955)
Reflections on Hanging (London, 1956)
The Sleepwalkers: A History of Man's Changing Vision of the Universe
    (London, 1959)
The Lotus and the Robot (London, 1960)
The Act of Creation (London, 1964)
The Ghost in the Machine (London, 1967)

The Drinkers of Infinity: Essays, 1956–1967 (London, 1968)
The Case of the Midwife Toad (London, 1971)
The Roots of Coincidence (London, 1972)
The Heel of Achilles: Essays 1968–1973 (London, 1974)
The Thirteenth Tribe (London, 1976)
Janus: A Summing Up (London, 1978)
Bricks to Babel (London, 1980)

Books by Koestler with Others

Wie ein Mangobaumwunder (Like a Mango Tree Miracle)
    (with Andor Németh) [1932] (Berlin, 1995)
The God that Failed: Six Studies in Communism (with Ignazio Silone,
    André Gide, Richard Wright, Louis Fischer and Stephen Spender),
    ed. Richard Crossman (London, 1950)
Beyond Reductionism: New Perspectives in the Life Sciences
    (ed. with J. R. Smythies) (London, 1969)
The Challenge of Chance: Experiments and Speculations
    (with Alister Hardy and Robert Harvie) (London, 1973)
Stranger on the Square (with Cynthia Koestler) (London, 1984)

Biographies & Memoirs

Buckard, Christian, *Koestler. Ein extremes Leben 1905–1983* (Munich, 2004)
Cesarani, David, *Arthur Koestler: The Homeless Mind* (London, 1998)
Hamilton, Iain, *Koestler: A Biography* (London, 1982)
Koestler, Mamaine, *Living with Koestler: Mamaine Koestler's Letters, 1945–51*,
    ed. Celia Goodman (New York, 1985)
Mikes, George, *Arthur Koestler: The Story of a Friendship* (London, 1983)
Németh, Andor, 'Memories of Koestler (Excerpts from a Memoir)',
    Hungarian Quarterly, CLLXVII (2005), pp. 11–22
Scammell, Michael, *Koestler: The Literary and Political Odyssey
    of a Twentieth-century Skeptic* (New York, 2009)
Strelka, Joseph, *Arthur Koestler: Autor – Kämpfer – Visionär*
    (Tübingen, 2006)

Criticism and Contexts

Arendt, Hannah, *The Origins of Totalitarianism* (New York, 1951)

Atkins, John, *Arthur Koestler* (London, 1956)

Beauvoir, Simone de, *The Mandarins*, trans. Leonard M. Friedman
(London, 1957)

Beller, Steven, ed., *Rethinking Vienna 1900* (New York and Oxford, 2001)

Berkowitz, Roger, 'Approaching Infinity: Dignity in Arthur Koestler's
Darkness at Noon', *Philosophy and Literature*, XXXIII/2 (2009),
pp. 296–314

Bloom, Harold, ed., *Arthur Koestler's 'Darkness at Noon'* (Broomall, PA, 2004)

Brockmann, Stephen, *German Literary Culture at the Zero Hour* (London, 2004)

Buber-Neumann, Margarete, *Under Two Dictators: Prisoner of Stalin and
Hitler*, trans. Edward Fitzgerald [1949] (London, 2008)

Christie, Agatha, *Passenger to Frankfurt* [1970] (London, 2003)

Clare, George, *Last Waltz in Vienna: The Destruction of a Family, 1842–1942*
(London, 1982)

Congdon, Lee, *Seeing Red: Hungarian Intellectuals in Exile and the Challenge
of Communism* (DeKalb, IL, 2001)

Duban, James, 'Arthur Koestler and Meyer Levin: The Trivial, the Tragic,
and Rationalization Post Factum in Roth's "Eli, the Fanatic"',
Philip Roth Studies, VII/2 (2011), pp. 171–86

—, '"Oceanic Wonder": Arthur Koestler and Melville's Castaway',
Philosophy and Literature, XXXV/2 (2011), pp. 371–4

—, '"That Butcher, Imagination": Arthur Koestler and the Bisociated
Narration of Philip Roth's Indignation', *Philip Roth Studies*, VIII/2
(2012), pp. 145–60

—, 'To Dazzle as Macbeth: Bisociated Drama in Philip Roth's
The Humbling', *Comparative Drama*, XLVI/1 (2012), pp. 1–16

Fallowell, Duncan, 'Arthur Koestler, The Art of Fiction No. 80', *Paris Review*,
XCII (1984)

Freadman, Richard, *Threads of a Life: Autobiography and the Will*
(Chicago, IL, 2001)

Grene, Marjorie, ed., 'Toward a Unity of Knowledge', *Psychological Issues*,
VI/2 (1969)

Harris, Harold, ed., *Astride the Two Cultures: Arthur Koestler at 70*
(London, 1975)

Harrison, Brian, *Seeking a Role: The United Kingdom, 1951–1970* (Oxford, 2011)

Howard, Elizabeth Jane, *Slipstream: A Memoir* (London, 2003)

Hughes, Langston, *Collected Works*, vol. xiv: *Autobiography: I Wonder as I Wander*, ed. Joseph McLaren (Columbia, mo, 2003)

Ignotus, Pál, and Arthur Koestler, '"The Contact has Always Remained": A Conversation Between Arthur Koestler and Pál Ignotus', *Hungarian Quarterly*, clxxvii (2005), pp. 23–5

Ignotus, Paul, 'The Hungary of Michael Polanyi', in *The Logic of Personal Knowledge. Essays Presented to Michael Polanyi on his Seventieth Birthday* (London, 1961), pp. 3–12

Judt, Tony, *Reappraisals. Reflections on the Forgotten Twentieth Century* (London, 2009), p. 40

Kirkham, Pat, Pat Moore and Pirco Wolfframm, eds, *Eva Zeisel: Life, Design, and Beauty* (San Francisco, ca, 2013)

Kuhn, Thomas S., *The Structure of Scientific Revolutions* [1962] (Chicago, il, and London, 2012)

Le Rider, Jacques, *Modernity and Crises of Identity: Culture and Society in Fin-de-siècle Vienna*, trans. Rosemary Morris (Cambridge, 1993)

Lukacs, John, *Budapest 1900: A Historical Portrait of a City and its Culture* (New York, 1988)

Merleau-Ponty, Maurice, *Humanism and Terror: An Essay on the Communist Problem*, trans. John O'Neill [1947] (Boston, ma, 1969)

Nye, Mary Jo, *Michael Polanyi and His Generation: Origins of the Social Construction of Science* (Chicago, il, 2011)

Polanyi, Michael, *Science, Faith and Society* [1949] (Chicago, 1964)

Popper, Karl, *The Logic of Scientific Discovery* [1935/1959] (London and New York, 2002)

—, *The Open Society and its Enemies* [1945] (London and New York, 2011)

Poulain, Martine, 'A Cold War Best-seller: The Reaction to Arthur Koestler's Darkness at Noon in France from 1945 to 1950', *Libraries and Culture*, xxxvi/1 (2001), pp. 172–84

Reynold, Nick, *Britain's Unfulfilled Mandate for Palestine* (London, 2014)

Richards, Jean, and Brent C. Brolin, eds, *Eva Zeisel: A Soviet Prison Memoir* (New York, 2012)

Richards, Robert J., *The Romantic Conception of Life: Science and Philosophy in the Age of Goethe* (Chicago, il, and London, 2002)

Rollyson, Carl, *A Private Life of Michael Foot* (Plymouth, 2015)

—, *To Be a Woman: The Life of Jill Craigie* (London, 2005)

Said, Edward, *The Question of Palestine* (London and Henley, 1980)

Sarkar, Sahotra, 'Models of Reduction and Categories of Reductionism', *Synthese*, XCI (1992), pp. 167–94

Silverman, Lisa, 'Reconsidering the Margins', *Journal of Modern Jewish Studies*, VIII/1 (2009), pp. 103–20

Snow, E. P., *The Two Cultures and a Second Look* (Cambridge, 1964)

Sperber, Murray, *Arthur Koestler: A Collection of Critical Essays* (Englewood Cliffs, NJ, 1977)

Stein, Leslie, *The Making of Modern Israel, 1948–1967* (Cambridge, 2009), pp. 37–8

Stonor Saunders, Frances, *Who Paid the Piper? The CIA and the Cultural Cold War* (London, 1999)

Taunton, Matthew, '2 +2 = 5: The Politics of Number in Writing about the Soviet Union', *Textual Practice*, XXIX/5 (2015), pp. 993–1016

Taussig Scott, William, and Martin X. Moleski, *Michael Polanyi: Scientist and Philosopher* (Oxford, 2005)

Weigel, Robert G., ed., *Arthur Koestler. Ein heller Geist in dunkler Zeit* (Tübingen, 2009)

Weissberg, Alex, *Conspiracy of Silence* (London, 1952)

Winkler, Martin M., ed., *Spartacus: Film and History* (Malden, MA, and Oxford, 2007)

Acknowledgements

The writing of this book was made possible by the generous support of the Ludwig Boltzmann Institute for the History and Theory of Biography and the Ludwig Boltzmann Gesellschaft.

The idea to write on Koestler originated in a discussion with the Institute's director, Wilhelm Hemecker, who also gave me the opportunity to come to Vienna. I am indebted to all of my other colleagues at the Institute for their insight and input, and especially to Tobias Heinrich and Katharina Prager, who helped shape my thinking in various ways. Lydia Morgan, Marie Kolkenbrock and Christopher Geissler were critical readers of related work. Thanks, too, to the advisory board and evaluators of the Institute for supporting and encouraging this project as it developed.

Without the patience and enthusiasm of Michael Leaman and all the team at Reaktion Books, this Critical Life would not have been possible. I am also grateful to all those who supported the research process or helped me with the images, particularly to Graeme Eddie at the University of Edinburgh Research Collections, and to Dmitrii Vasil'ev, John Hartsock, Matthias Weßel, Jean Richards and Mikhail Shifman for their interest from afar.

In particular, I would like to say a big thank you to my sister, Tess, for her proofreading of the manuscript, as well as to all my Vienna friends and visitors: Anne and Nick, Cornelius and Sarah, Roman and Teresa, Felix and Emily, Kate and Catherine, Lena, Maria, Hannah, Raphaela, Stefan, Marlene, Elisabeth and Saif, Cäcilie, Tanya, Gruia, Jurij, Charlotte, Anja and Gordon, Fabi and, last but not least, Rupert. The Trimmel family has looked after me and helped me out often. Mum and Dad, there is so much of your influence in this book. Wolfgang, words cannot express how much I owe to you.

Lastly, although they will probably never read this book, I'd like to thank all my students at the Austrian Red Cross, whose biographies helped me put Koestler's life (and my own) into perspective: Ahmad, Shams, Saidreza, Wahid, Asabuddain, Mohammad Rafi, Amir Mohamad and Bashir.

Photo Acknowledgements

The author and publishers wish to express their thanks to the below sources of illustrative material and/or permission to reproduce it.

L'Amicale des anciens internés politiques et résistants du camp de concentration du vernet d'Ariège: p. 59; Bildarchiv Austria/Österreichische Nationalbibliothek, Vienna: pp. 21, 26, 139; bpk/IMEC, Fonds MCC/Gisèle Freund: p. 8; photo © The British Library Board: p. 159; Bundesarchiv, Koblenz: p. 47; Edinburgh University Library: pp. 71, 81; Pat English/ Getty Images: p. 88; Eva Zeisel Archive: pp. 16, 32, 48; The Koestler Trust: p. 171; Gerry McCann/Alamy: p. 155; Wolfgang Pfaundler/Europäisches Forum Alpbach: p. 106; ullstein bild: p. 35; ullstein bild/Karoly Forgacs: p. 105; United News/Popperfoto/Getty Images: p. 163; UPI/Süddeutsche Zeitung Photo: p. 93.